Christian Spirituality

SCM CORE TEXT

Christian Spirituality

Karen E. Smith

scm press

British Library Cataloguing in Publication data

A catalogue record for this book is available
from the British Library

978 0 334 04042 2

First published in 2007 by SCM Press
13–17 Long Lane,
London EC1A 9PN

www.scm-canterburypress.co.uk

SCM Press is a division of
SCM-Canterbury Press Ltd

Typeset by Regent Typesetting
Printed and bound in Great Britain by
William Clowes Ltd, Beccles, Suffolk

Contents

For
E. Glenn Hinson

Preface

In many ways, I feel as if I have tried to write a book that cannot be written. It is not possible to find the words to express the various dimensions of Christian spirituality. In my struggle to write this introductory text, however, I have consoled myself that this book was not intended as a book to say everything, but merely to introduce certain themes and ideas. My main goal was to offer students some insight into the way that belief and experience interact when they are brought together by a desire to know and to be known by God.

I am aware that I have omitted many things that others would consider of vital importance. Specialists will feel that I have skirted over many issues that needed careful and close attention. I can only say that this is not a book for seasoned theologians, but for beginners in the field. Hence I have tried to keep the language simple and have tried to point to some of the deeper issues without delving too far into them. I wanted to write about Christian spirituality in a way that would be interesting and readable for anyone. So I have avoided the 'technical language' of the specialist and when it has been necessary to use such language, I have explained its meaning in the text rather than in a separate glossary. I am aware that some of the quotes that I have included in this book do not use inclusive language. Where possible I have put a word in brackets to show that the writer intended to include both men and women. However, some of the quotes are left untouched, especially if it seemed that the inclusion of bracketed words would 'clutter' the quotation and prevent the reader from engaging with the text.

Students wishing to go further in their exploration of Christian spirituality will want to consult the books I have noted in the further reading lists at the end of each chapter and in the glossary of Christian devotional writers that I have included at the end of the book. These are works that discuss some of the aspects of the study of spirituality with far more eloquence and depth than I could ever achieve.

Finally, while this is a core text for Christian spirituality, I see this book not so much as a textbook which will provide clear-cut answers to questions, but rather as an invitation to discovery. I hope you will receive it as such and read the chapters as if they were signposts pointing out key features on the journey rather than a map intended to give concrete directions or extensive discussions about every pothole or curve in the road. If when you have finished the book, you want to know more, I will have achieved my aim!

Acknowledgements

Although I have taught classes on Christian spirituality for many years, I think I have always realized that it was not a 'subject' which can be 'taught'. Rather, each group of students have seemed like fellow travellers who were there to explore what at times seems to be a strange and distant land. I have enjoyed the explorations with them and acknowledge my debt to all the students past and present who have been willing to share their insights with me. My thanks to Sue Beverly, Mike Arnold, Rhiannon Shuff, and Richard Sherlock for their willingness to read and comment on the Introduction.

I am grateful to others with whom I share work and life. My community of faith, Orchard Place Baptist Church in Neath, has been a place of belonging where I have been challenged to continue to discover and to celebrate the many dimensions of Christian spirituality. I am grateful to them for graciously allowing me to have a six-month sabbatical in order to do some of the writing. Charles and Barbara Clarke have offered me much encouragement. Charles served as pastoral friend to the congregation while I was on sabbatical and I am grateful to them both for their support and help.

My friends and colleagues in the South Wales Baptist College, John Weaver, Roy Kearsley, Martyn Moss, and Simon Woodman, have facilitated the writing of this book in different ways. I am particularly grateful to Simon who took time to read a draft of the chapter on story, made some helpful comments on narrative approaches to the Bible and pointed me in the direction of some recent literature on the subject. Many other friends have shared the journey with me and reminded me of what it means to 'bear one another's burdens'. My thanks in particular to Craig Gardiner who read the entire manuscript and offered criticism and suggestions. Helen Reynolds read the text with care and attention before the final typescript was prepared for the publisher. I would also like to thank Barbara Laing at SCM Press for her kindness and patience with me as I asked for several extensions of the deadline for the manuscript! While I gladly acknowledge the help and collaboration of colleagues and friends, I accept that any shortcomings of the book are my own.

My greatest debt is to my family. My husband, Paul Harris, has read the chapters in his usual perceptive, astute way and has offered helpful insights and critique. Paul, together with our boys, Taylor and Caleb (and Rusty, our Springer Spaniel), have supported me throughout this project. Without their friendship, love and support this book would not have been written.

Finally my thanks to my mentor and friend, E. Glenn Hinson, who introduced me to different expressions of Christian spirituality in a seminary class he taught on the Classics of Christian Devotion. Some of the chapters of this book grew out of a series of lectures I gave in his honour at the E. Glenn Hinson Institute for Spiritual Formation, at the Advent Spirituality Retreat Week in June 2002. I now dedicate this book to him with deep gratitude and appreciation.

Introduction: Christian Spiritualities

A Story . . . It has been told before, perhaps you have heard it: a story of a traveller.

It began in the beginning. That is, her search was from as early as she was, or at least as she can remember. The longing, for that is what the search was, took her to many places. She talked to kinfolk and stranger alike, but she never seemed to find the goal or object of her search. What was she looking for? Some said it was a 'pearl of great price' or a 'treasure in a field'. Others said she wanted to know and to be known by God. The traveller was not sure where the restless desire was taking her, but she believed that if she gave herself to the longing ultimately if she was to be found or to find, it would be the same.

After a while, the traveller grew tired of her restless longing and decided that she must stop looking and simply be content. She concentrated on her work, a job she liked, and felt successful. In the evenings, she watched television or went out with friends. Life was OK. She was happy. Yet, she was not content. And before long, she began to search again. Driven by desire (for that is what it was) she found herself in a bookstore looking up and down the shelves for some answers.

Sitting down in the shop with a cappuccino, she looked through a selection of books on 'spirituality'. The titles reflected an interest in all kinds of subjects that related to the 'spiritual' side of life. There were books on holistic living and healthy lifestyles, meditation and reflexology. She looked along the shelves, and came to a section on Christian spirituality. Some of these books sounded a bit bizarre, with titles like: 'Go Green with Jesus' and 'Be an Eco-Warrior for Christ'. Was spirituality about caring for the environment? She wasn't sure. Another book was entitled: 'Riding into Revelation: The Apocalypse Explained'. She opened it warily and quickly put it down again. The book seemed to be filled with strange stories about dragons, beasts and the great whore of Babylon! She went to another shelf and found a book was entitled, 'Power Driven by Christ'. The author of this book claimed that 'spirituality is all that I do' . . . 'it is the whole of life'. The traveller thought about her recent activities: meals with friends, DVDs she had watched, the argument she had with a colleague at work. Did spirituality include all her activities?

After an afternoon of browsing through the titles of books, the traveller was feeling very puzzled. Some of the books made it sound like Christian spirituality was about what a person believes about Jesus. Other books said it was about feeling close to Jesus. Some of the books suggested that spirituality had something to do with prayer or 'the spirit' or the inner development of a person. As she left the bookstore, she decided she would have to go and meet some people who claimed to be Christians. Perhaps then she would discover what Christian spirituality was all about.

She set off on her journey and one day she met a Very Religious Person (VRP) who showed her a great big black book. It was filled with many wise sayings and wonderful stories. The traveller liked the book very much and began to read it with great interest. When she began to talk to VRP about the stories and how they were to be interpreted, VRP stopped her and said with great solemnity, 'there is only one meaning'. And then, to the traveller's surprise, VRP pulled out a long list of rules and regulations and began to read them to the traveller. 'This is the official understanding of all that is in the black book', said VRP. 'There is no need to read the book and try to interpret it yourself. In fact, you cannot read and interpret the stories for yourself. Simply read these statements and believe.' The traveller was very sad and confused, too. She had so many questions which were not answered by the long list of rules.

Eventually she decided to travel on. This time she came to another Very Religious Person (VRP2) who seemed very happy. In fact she seemed unable to speak without interjecting 'Praise the Lord' or 'Hallelujah' or some other loud exaltation into the conversation. The conversation began as VRP2 asked the traveller if (Hallelujah, Thank You Jesus) she had experienced anything on the way. 'Well I have had many experiences of love and happiness,' said the traveller. 'I have known many people who have taught me about life.' 'No, no', cried VRP2, 'I don't mean (Thank You Jesus) those kinds of things (Praise the Lord!), I mean (Sweet Lord) special experiences of God and God's spirit (Thank You Jesus).' 'I am not sure what you mean,' said the traveller. 'I have felt the wind blow on my face, and I have sat alone by the sea and known I was not alone. I have sensed in so many deep ways that I belong to something or someone beyond me. And sometimes, I have seen the tears in the eyes of a stranger. I have sensed the joy of others and sometimes their pain and known that we belonged to each other.' VRP2 looked at the traveller impatiently. 'No, no (Hallelujah)', she cried, 'I don't mean general kinds of experiences. I mean have you specifically felt a sweet walk with God (Thank You Lord)? Have you (Praise the Lord) felt that God was speaking to you? Have you (Thank You Jesus) prayed the sinner's prayer? Have you sung songs loudly enough for all to hear and waved your hands in the air to express your new-found freedom (Amen, Hallelujah)? If you do these things', VRP2 said, 'and you have a sweet experience when your heart is strangely warmed (Hallelujah), you will know that you were lost and now (Praise the Lord) you have been found.' The traveller felt confused. She liked VRP2. She liked her exuberance and felt there was something quite genuine about her life. Yet, the traveller knew that she could not accept what VRP2 was saying. VRP2's experience could not be her experience. The traveller had experienced many things in life, but could not seem to relate to what VRP2 was saying, so she decided to travel on.

The traveller came to a village and stopped by the gate of a church and, sitting down on a bench to rest, she watched as someone who obviously was another Very Religious Person (VRP3), walked through the gate and into the church. Wondering what was happening in the church building, the traveller made her way to the door. Inside, she saw VRP3 on his knees and muttering something like . . . 'Hello, Mary'. The traveller was confused, as she did not see anyone else in the building. Where was this Mary and why did VRP3 keep speaking to her? Looking around the building, the traveller was quite impressed with the statues and stained-glass windows. The place seemed to smell different. It was unusual and somehow quite special. She decided to wait until VRP3 had finished speaking to whoever he was speaking to and have a word with VRP3 herself. At last, VRP3 finished and stood up and in spite of the fact that the traveller had been there for some time VRP3 seemed not to notice. 'Excuse me', said the traveller, 'excuse me, please.' VRP3 turned and looked at his watch and then at the traveller. 'I wonder if I can have a word with you? I have been walking the road for some time. I am being guided by a deep longing. Sometimes, I feel as if I am being pushed and sometimes it is as if I am being called, yes that is it, I am being beckoned forward, it is hard to explain and I am not sure what I am looking for. I wonder if you can help me?' VRP3 looked at his watch again and said: 'I am not sure I can help you. You should see the priest about things like that. I imagine he will direct you to a good retreat or perhaps suggest that you begin with daily Eucharist or weekly Mass. You should follow the missal carefully. But of course, you would need catechetical instruction first in order to have a complete understanding of the sacrificial and atoning death of the Christ, our blessed Lord, whose mother was Mary, the virgin, the most blessed and righteous one.' The traveller was startled and a bit confused. Eucharist? Missal? Retreat? Mary, the virgin? She had no idea what VRP3 was talking about and quickly turned to get away.

When she was back on the road, she met yet another Very Religious

Person (VRP4) who was standing at the side of the road, handing out invitations to a service at her local church. She smiled at the traveller and made her feel that she would be very welcome. 'I hope to see you there to-night', she said to the traveller. It was getting late, so the traveller decided she would stop for the night and go along to the service. Perhaps here she would find the answer to her restless longing. When she arrived at the church she saw a group of men waiting at the door. She thought that perhaps they were 'bouncers' like the ones who stand outside the local bars, and she wondered if they would try to keep her from going inside. Cautiously, she went to the door and, to her surprise, they welcomed her. She went inside and sat down. People gathered at the front and led the people who were sitting in chairs in singing lively songs. They had a big screen at the front of the building and on it they had the words to songs. They had prayers and then a person started talking about 'doing things' for God. He read from the big black book and then he spoke for a long time about the use of things: time, money, talents, and more money. The sermon, as it was called, went on for quite a while. At the end the travel-ler felt sad because apparently she had not done enough for God. When she left, she felt quite worried. She could not simply believe the rules, she had not had the right kind of experience, she did not go on retreats, and obviously she was not up to all the work that seemed to be required.

A few days later, as she walked along the road, the traveller met a fel-low traveller who said that she had been travelling along the Way for many years. 'Are you a Religious Person?', asked the traveller of her com-panion. 'Oh I don't know', she said, 'I think I gave up on religion years ago. I am more interested in relationship than religion.' This sounded interesting to the traveller who asked her companion to say more. 'Well', said the fellow traveller, 'I think that God is in God's self relationship, and we are all made to be like God and to long for relationship with God and with one another. Spirituality, if that is what we should call it,' she said, 'is about loving God and loving people, nothing more and nothing less.' 'What about the big black book and what about the list of rules and regulations?' 'The book, God gives to be read and studied', said the fellow traveller, 'and sometimes we make for ourselves lists of do's and don'ts, but following the Way is not about what we know about God. Perhaps it is as much about not knowing as knowing.'

'What kind of experience should I have so that I know I am part of the Way?' asked the traveller. The fellow traveller smiled and said: 'There are many kinds of experiences and there are many different ways of knowing and being known.' At this point the traveller looked confused. 'So what am I to do? How am I to move forward on the Way to God?' At this her fellow traveller looked at her and said: 'The Way is not to be found in a particular set of doctrines or in a particular kind of experience. The Way will be discovered as you allow knowledge to converse with experience. When what you think you know challenges your experience, you must embrace the challenge. When your experience challenges what you believe to be true about faith, you must allow the experience to renew your tired old ideas. Most of all be open and continue to give yourself to the desire to know and to be known. As you give yourself to the longing you will discover that knowing is in not knowing. As you listen intently to the conversation between doctrine and experience, you will discover that you are being changed: transfigured and transformed.' And with that, the two travellers continued their journey down the road together. They knew that they would not always be together. Later they would meet other travellers who would tell them about where they had been and stories of others who had journeyed with them. They would be encouraged by some of the tales and challenged by others. And they would tell their stories. And maybe listen to yours, too.

What is spirituality?

This is a book about stories. It is about your story, my story and the stories of others, as well as the story of God. At the heart of Christian spirituality there is one central story of Jesus Christ: his birth, death and resurrection. Christian spirituality is not about simply hearing the story and believing it to be true, of course. It is also about experiencing relationship with Christ. This is one reason why it is difficult to explain Christian spirituality. Because, as the traveller discovered, there are many different ways of interpreting Christian faith in human experience.

The story of the traveller is a parody which exaggerates certain viewpoints and rituals, but the fact remains that there are extreme differences in doctrine and practice among Christians. Unfortunately, at times some Christians have excluded others on the basis of differences in belief. Others have looked for assurances of particular kinds of experiences. And using labels such as liberal, evangelical, conservative, liturgical, traditional, 'high' or 'low' church, Protestant and Catholic, there are fixed stereotypes of what Christians of one caste or another must be like.

The inclusion of so many facets of life and so many approaches to Christian faith under the heading 'spirituality' makes it very hard to pin down a meaning for the word. Does a person need to believe in God or another realm of life after death to claim an approach to spirituality? Is spirituality simply about life and the way we live it? If so, how does that differ from a study of ethics? Is spirituality about discovering our true selves and relating to others? If so, how does this differ from the study of psychology or sociology? Is it necessary to make a distinction between the spiritual and material? Does spirituality demand belief in particular doctrines or is it primarily about experience? The answers to these questions and others will lead inevitably to very different ways of understanding spirituality.

This book explores the nature of Christian spirituality through several recurring themes found in Christian writings across the centuries. However, the purpose is not to offer a precise definition of Christian spirituality nor simply to give an account of approaches to spirituality, but to point to the way that different understandings of doctrine or beliefs and varied experiences of life and faith together may form very different patterns in the rich and varied tapestry of Christian spirituality.

Writing from a Christian perspective, John O'Donohue claims that 'spirituality is the art of transfiguration'.[1] He may be right and perhaps this is why spirituality itself seems to elude definition. Christian spirituality, much like art or music, is not simply a subject to be studied. Rather it must be engaged and explored. It is not easily defined, because it does not easily submit to interpretation. It cannot be approached in the way one might tackle and solve a mathematical problem. That is to say, it cannot be inspected and discussed in purely analytical terms in order to arrive at a conclusion. Rather, Christian spirituality is discovered and explored, shaped and formed, in the context of an ongoing engagement between belief (or unbelief) and experience. This does not mean, of course, that an individual needs to confess certain Christian doctrines or have an experience of Christian faith in order to study spirituality. But it does mean that the person who embarks on the study of Christian spirituality must look carefully at the ideas and beliefs, as well as the experiences claimed by individual Christians and their communities of faith. This approach affirms the need to listen to the stories of others and to live with the uncertainty of questions rather than simply offering answers.

Some Christians may find this approach to spirituality rather uncomfortable. Like some of the VRPs in the traveller's tale, some people want to feel that they have 'the answer' or have had 'the experience': case closed, questions answered. Yet many people, especially those who want to describe our era as 'postmodern', find it difficult to take for granted the assurances of the Enlightenment period. That is to say, they do not feel, for instance, that humankind is steadily moving forward and progressing on the basis of reason and objective truth. The so called 'postmodernists' would argue that truth is far more elusive and can't simply be discovered.

While it is helpful to think about how we understand our age, we should be suspicious of the terms 'modern' and 'postmodern' when it comes to speaking about life and faith. To label and categorize ways of thinking immediately limits our thoughts.

As we shall see, the elusiveness of a defining statement for Christian spirituality has as much to do with the nature of Christian experience as it does with postmodern thought. Among the first Christian believers, it was evident that not all Christians shared the same belief or experience of God, and New Testament writers – for example, the Apostle Paul – openly stated that knowledge of God and faith was only partial and could not be fully expressed.

As we explore both belief and experience among the followers of Christ, it is arguable that Christian spirituality is at best a reflection of the love of God which, by its very nature, cannot be defined in terms of a particular doctrine(s) or set of beliefs or any one particular experience. Christians believe that the love of God was revealed to us in the life, death and resurrection of Jesus Christ and is continually discovered anew through the power of God as Holy Spirit. Awareness of the infinite boundless reaches of the height, depth and breadth of God's love is an ongoing discovery made in relationship with God, others and creation. The various expressions of Christian spirituality are mere reflections of our very partial understanding and experience of that love. As the Apostle Paul wrote: 'For now we see in a mirror dimly, but then we will see face to face. Now I know in part; then I will know fully, even as I have been fully known' (1 Corinthians 13.12).

Hence, while Christian spirituality may not be explained and labelled, neither may it be defined by a system of beliefs, or described in terms of certain practices. Moreover, it is not simply all that we are in the world. It is in fact more than what we can ever experience in the world – it embraces hope for a different world and points to both thought and action which, as Christian faith teaches, reflects the very heart of a God of love. While it is possible to describe some aspects of Christian spirituality, any engagement between (un)belief and experience will in fact leave us with the feeling that 'it is much more than it is'.[2]

Ways of approaching Christian spirituality

Although Christian faith may not be easily categorized, over the years Christian spirituality has often been studied from one of these two vantage points: doctrine or experience. While a clear division between the two allows us to grapple with various themes or topics in Christian spirituality, it actually encourages the false idea that spirituality is related to *either* doctrine *or* experience. As the traveller in the opening story discovered, sometimes there is an emphasis on knowing certain doctrines and at other times there may be an emphasis on having a certain type of experience. In fact, an exploration of spirituality embraces both intellectual knowledge and experience or to put it another way, an understanding of God and an awareness of the transcendent. Moreover, an exploration of spirituality should not be limited to any individual's particular understanding of Christian doctrine and experience, but looks for conversation with the wider beliefs and experiences of others within the Christian tradition.

Not all Christians hold identical beliefs, nor have they had identical experiences. In fact, people tend to place varying degrees of importance on particular beliefs or experiences. For some, for instance, a 'conversion' experience is a clearly identifiable point in time when one turned to God in repentance. Others prefer to speak of conversion as a gradual process. Some people in fact may find it difficult to speak in terms of a conversion, but prefer to describe times of new-found peace or moments of enlightenment or perhaps they simply describe a sense of new orientation emerging from a period of disorientation.[3] Some place greater emphasis on particular texts of the Bible, others stress a particular doctrine or relate a particular experience. All of these variations in belief and experience highlight the need to speak of Christian spiritualities rather than Christian spirituality.

There are Christians who would dispute this claim. Some people argue that Christian faith is built on a foundation of certain beliefs and, for them, spirituality must be based on right belief (orthodoxy). Those who think of spirituality in terms of right belief will sometimes speak of types of spirituality in a way that reflects particular doctrinal ideas, that is Roman Catholic, Lutheran, Anglican, Methodist, Baptist, etc. The assumption is that within these denominational groupings there is broad agreement on particular doctrines of faith, which shapes the experience or expression of spirituality. While doctrinal and traditional views most certainly shape Christian spirituality, this approach tends to ignore the fact that there is great variety of opinion and thought even within denominations. There is an old joke which says that if you put three Baptists in a room together to discuss their understanding of doctrine, you will discover that they have at least five or six opinions. I am sure that the same will be said of Roman Catholics, Methodists, Anglicans or any other denominational group. Does this mean that Christians, even within the same tradition, can display a variety of beliefs and that there isn't one set of doctrines to which all Christians adhere? The answer, quite simply, is yes. At any point in history there has been a broad spectrum of belief within the Church, with there being perhaps as many spiritualities as there are Christians. History is full of conflicts and persecution within the Church which reflect the desire of some to force uniformity in belief or practice.

In looking for a way of exploring Christian spirituality, it may be suggested that if we do not begin with doctrine, we should begin with the perspective of experience. Those who think of spirituality in this way categorize it through an apparent common practice or concern; spirituality is described as contemplative, evangelical, radical, feminist, etc. While this allows for a broad discussion of approaches to the practice of Christian devotion, it should not be assumed that even within these categories there is uniformity of experience. This is evident, for instance, if one contrasts feminist spirituality with the approach of those writing from a womanist perspective.[4] Nor can it be assumed that one type sums up the whole of a person's approach. Nor does it mean that categories are mutually exclusive. The concerns indicated by a particular category may not be the only shaping influence on a person's approach to spirituality. It is, for example, possible for a person's approach to spirituality to be feminist, evangelical, contemplative and much more besides!

A further difficulty with approaching spirituality through experience is that it seems to imply that spirituality is a skill to be acquired or a task to be accomplished. This is typified in the popular self-help, 'how-to' style of many books on spirituality. The impression one has from those who emphasize method or approach is that spirituality is all about doing things, that is praying, meditating, etc. and that there is one way (a right way as opposed to a wrong way) of approaching these tasks. This approach to spirituality seems to focus on religion and religious experience as a learned and practised behaviour. While there are undeniably some ritual practices within the Christian religion that may provide individuals with a way of expressing their devotion, which is helpful and meaningful to them, spirituality is not measured by the ability to perform religious acts of ritual. Moreover, given the wide variety of types of ritual it would be impossible to isolate any one particular practice as the measure to Christian spirituality. To give one unusual example, there are Christians living in the Appalachian Mountains in America who believe that a ritual act of communal foot-washing must be practised before they come to the Lord's Table. This practice is based on the belief that according to the Gospel of John, Jesus washed his disciples' feet before they shared a meal together and then said to his disciples, 'So if I, your Lord and Teacher, have washed your feet, you also ought to wash one another's feet' (John 13.14). Those who practise this custom would claim that it is essential to Christian spirituality. That is to say, they would not share in the Lord's Supper unless they had washed each other's feet. Clearly, other Christians would not hold this to be true. There are many other differences in the approach to worship, for example, which point to the great diversity of practice within Christian faith and highlight the impossibility of rooting Christian spirituality in the practice of particular traditions, ceremonies or ritual acts.

In addition to the impossibility of finding uniformity among Christians in either doctrinal belief or experience, there is one further difficulty which occurs if one tries to approach spirituality from the perspective of orthopraxy (correct action) or orthodoxy (correct belief). The two are inextricably linked. They are intertwined and interwoven in life with one belief or experience shaping other beliefs or experiences. That is why, for instance, some have resorted to making the claim that spirituality is all of life – it is the whole of what one believes and experiences. Yet, this claim in fact is not strictly true. Christian spirituality may not be all that I experience or believe. To say that spirituality is merely what I know and understand is to place a boundary on what Christians believe to be without limit: the love of God.

Dialogue between doctrine and experience

If one cannot assume that Christian spirituality may be understood by looking at either doctrine or practice, and if it is too broad a claim to suggest that spirituality is all that I believe and practise, how then may it be described? The approach that we shall take is that Christian spiritualities are discovered as individuals and groups engage in an ongoing conversation between doctrine and experience. The conversation focuses on what we believe or think we believe about religious faith and what we have experienced of life. It might also be shaped by our impressions of the beliefs and experiences of others. This conversation is always in progress. At times an individual may think that she has arrived at a clear understanding of Christian spirituality only to discover that a new experience, or perhaps the reflection on another person's experience, calls into question what was first believed and the conversation between belief and experience is held again. To put it another way, just when a person feels at home with a particular doctrine, experience may tap on the door of belief or vice versa and the conversation between doctrine and experience begins again.

Let me explain by way of a personal story. I was brought up in a conservative evangelical faith tradition which emphasized an optimistic and convinced Christian faith. I learned that relationship with God was possible because of the unmerited favour of God shown to individuals in the gift of his son Jesus Christ. I was taught from a very young age to believe in a loving God, who like a good father watches over all his children. This approach to Christian faith encouraged me to do certain things: engage with Scripture, pray and attend worship services regularly. It also suggested to me that it is important to avoid smoking, drinking alcohol, or swearing and to generally try to live in a way that is kind and helpful. This type of faith tradition seemed to emphasize certainty rather than uncertainty, so, not surprisingly, most of my experience of God simply confirmed what I already believed to be true from my experience of life: God was a good God; faithful, loving and kind toward me, my family and all who believed as we did.

When I was 19 this belief was brought into question for me when I found myself feeling abandoned by God in an intensive-care ward of a hospital. Out of this experience of suffering and isolation, I began to question my understanding of the nature of God and God's purposes for humankind. In fact, I even questioned whether God actually existed or was simply the product of my imagination or at least simply the reflection of a collection of beliefs which were as much a part of the culture I was brought up in as anything else. Was it necessary to believe in God? Was there a God or was God simply a construct which humankind needed or felt they needed? These questions and others formed the basis of an ongoing dialogue between faith and experience which I believe is at the heart of any approach to Christian spirituality.

My experience, which is by no means unique, is an illustration of what happens when belief and experience seem dissonant and apart from one another; belief and experience confront one another and the need for dialogue between the two is apparent. One does not of course need to begin at the point of belief. There are numerous examples in the Christian tradition of those who began from a point of unbelief. While holding firmly to an agnostic stance with regard to Christian faith, there are many stories of men and women who had an experience which challenged their unbelief. For Dorothy Day, the founder of the Catholic Worker Movement, it was the birth of a child and her desire to thank God.[5] For C. S. Lewis, it was while riding a bus in Oxford that he suddenly realized that he had a choice to make. He described it in this way:

> The odd thing was that before God closed in on me, I was in fact offered what now appears a moment of wholly free choice. In a sense. I was going up Headington Hill on the top of a bus. Without words and (I think) almost without images, a fact about myself was somehow presented to me. I became aware that I was holding something at bay, or shutting something out. Or, if you like, that I was wearing some stiff clothing, like corsets, or even a suit of armour, as if I were a lobster. I felt myself being, there and then, given a free choice. I could open the door or keep it shut; I could unbuckle the armour or keep it on.[6]

For others the decision to embrace Christian spirituality came after a difficult life experience. Ignatius of Loyola, the founder of the Society of Jesus (Jesuits) in the sixteenth century, began to explore Christian faith more deeply as he was recuperating after being wounded in the battle of Pampeluna in 1521. He began reading the life of Christ and the biographies of the saints and felt he was being drawn to follow in the way of Christ.

While conversation between doctrine and experience is often brought to the fore in a crisis situation, in fact the type of interchange which takes place when experience challenges belief or (un)belief challenges experience is the kind of discourse which is at the core of any religious experience. Recognition that life experience may not be separated from religious belief, or to put it another way, that religious experience is not necessarily different from life experience, has opened the door to other tools which aid the exploration of Christian spirituality.

Social sciences and spirituality

The study of psychology, which is devoted to the examination of human behaviour and personality, and sociology, which explores aspects of order, structure and relationship within communities, have offered many helpful insights into the study religion. While some Christians appear to be fearful that religious faith will be reduced to little more than a psychological mind game, or social construct, others have acknowledged the helpfulness of looking carefully at shaping influences on spirituality such as personality type, familial ties and cultural conditioning.

Likewise, those who have studied human growth and developing patterns of behaviour have brought rich insight into the way one may approach Christian faith. James Fowler, for instance, has usefully examined the way individuals sometimes hold to a particular set of beliefs in a pattern that is reminiscent of an adolescent stage of human growth and development which desires conformity. More recently, Nicola Slee has examined the experience of women and suggested that while Fowler's approach takes human experience seriously, there is scope for further study of the rich and varied patterns of women's faith development.[7] Significantly, though, both Fowler and Slee point to the fact that at a certain point in faith development there is often a willingness to allow doctrine to be challenged by experience and vice versa. For Fowler this often happens when one is able to embrace paradox. The movement through particular 'stages of faith' or recognition of 'emerging patterns' of faith development often depends on the ability or willingness of an individual to allow one's doctrine or belief to enter into dialogue with one's experience. And it is as the conversation takes place that Christian spirituality is discovered in new ways or perhaps shaped and formed or re-formed and even transfigured over and over again.

The fields of psychology and sociology are an important means for exploring religious human experience. In the late nineteenth and early part of the twentieth centuries, Sigmund Freud, the 'father of psychoanalysis', put forward theories about psychosexual development and the development of personality. His ideas, particularly relating to dream analysis, were taken up by C. G. Jung, who, while being impressed with Freud's sexual theory, was doubtful about Freud's tendency to see things related to spirituality as 'repressed sexuality'.[8] Jung was the son of a Swiss Protestant pastor and six of his mother's brothers were clergymen. So it is not surprising that Jung had a deep interest in religious experience. He was, however, suspicious of religious systems. Jungian analysis, particularly as it relates to dreams and his approach to personality types, has been used to explore faith development and to examine approaches to spirituality.[9]

Some Christians, of course, feel that psychology should not be brought into any discussion of faith. However, one does not need to simply dismiss religious belief in Freudian terms as a 'dream wish fulfilment' or to accept that faith is merely a product of cultural conditioning. Moreover, those who ultimately claim to hold to belief in God and do so within the framework of Christian faith do not necessarily affirm that religious belief ensures that life will be free of mental, emotional or physical pain or difficulty. In fact, many would acknowledge that sometimes the sharper experiences of pain, suffering, and/or disappointment which are at the heart of human relationship may draw us into a deeper understanding of God.

The suffering experienced in life may be explored as part of a belief in a God, who, in the cross, has embraced and experienced suffering. The mystery of a God who suffers is at the heart of Christian faith and part of the Christian doctrine of God which is expressed as a Trinity or one God in three persons: Creator, Redeemer, Sustainer. This way of imagining God is in part a reminder in Christian theology that at the heart of belief in the mystery of the suffering of God is the experience of relationship.[10] While we will look briefly at the themes of suffering and relationship in community in later chapters, it is important to note here that the idea of God in community highlights the fact that the dialogue between doctrine and experience takes place in the context of relationship. Individual (un)belief is never held simply in isolation. Rather, belief and experience are shaped and formed within the particular context in which we find ourselves and patterns of faith emerge out of the inter-wovenness of our lives with the lives of others.

Stories of faith

Since all life is lived in the context of relationships, it is not surprising that one approach to the study of Christian spirituality is through biography.[11] As the study of an artist or composer may provide greater insight into a piece of art or music, the exploration of spirituality through biography enables one to learn something of the context in which that expression of faith developed. That is not to say, of course, that mere knowledge of an individual's life will enable one to understand a particular expression of spirituality; just as knowledge of the artist's or composer's life or intent within their work will not take the place of an individual's own experience of the artwork or composition. Similarly, knowing about the beliefs and experiences of Christian faith will not lead one to an exact belief or experience; rather like what happens in an experience of art when each person's engagement with a work leads to an interpretation or experience that is uniquely their own.

Although the life of any individual might be examined, in order to explore spirituality, in the history of the Christian tradition it has been generally recognized that the lives and writings of certain Christians offer rich insight into the nature of faith. The body of literature which includes biographies and autobiographies, as well as collections of sayings and devotional directives from Christian writers, has become known as the classics of Christian devotion. The classics are wide-ranging over many centuries of Christian belief, including, for example, the writings of the

Desert Fathers and Mothers, St Augustine of Hippo, Mother Julian of Norwich, the seventeenth-century Puritan John Bunyan, as well as more modern writers such as the Quaker Thomas Kelly or the Roman Catholic Thomas Merton and many others besides. Naturally one cannot identify one particular approach to Christian spirituality among these writers.

The writers vary widely in their doctrinal understanding and demonstrate the great variety of experience within the Christian tradition. Some, for instance, speak of the necessity of regular patterns of prayer and the importance of silence. Others highlight the need for engagement with the world, particularly in matters of justice and equality. What is significant, of course, is that an examination of these writings provides the opportunity for the reader to explore the interplay between belief and experience.

Spirituality: more than doctrine or experience

Up to this point, we have highlighted two very important aspects of Christian spirituality, namely doctrine and experience, and suggested that the study of spirituality requires a willingness to engage in conversation between the two. This kind of interchange is very closely aligned to the type of engagement between 'religious belief, tradition, and practice when it meets contemporary experiences, questions and actions' in the discipline of practical theology or pastoral theology.[12] For this reason, sometimes the study of spirituality is included in courses on practical theology. However, it may be argued that those who are exploring spirituality are engaged in a study that, while it is not entirely separate, is, in fact, different from that of the practical theologian. This difference is noted by Marie McCarthy when she speaks of 'the gift of spirituality to practical and pastoral theology' and claims that practical and pastoral theologies are enriched by the study of spirituality. She writes:

> The study of spirituality is never merely an intellectual exercise. It draws one in. It demands an active participation . . . We begin to understand not just with our minds, but with our hearts and our very beings and we begin to reflect in our lives that which we study.[13]

The sense of being 'drawn in' and engaging with our very beings, in an 'active participation', as McCarthy puts it, is a vital part of the study of spirituality. While one may not claim that it is exclusive to spirituality (one might equally feel drawn and engaged and even transformed by a study of Reformation history or philosophy) McCarthy is right to point out that the study of spirituality is not simply an examination of 'religious belief, tradition, and practice when it meets contemporary experiences, questions and actions', but it also pays close attention to a deeper imperative. This imperative is what we might call desire or longing.

While it is difficult to describe, a sense of longing or desire is at the root of every expression of Christian spirituality. In many ways it appears that it is desire which enables the conversation between belief and experience to take place. What is this longing? It is described in different ways: a desire in life for happiness, for peace. Ultimately perhaps it is related to a search for meaning. However one may describe it, as Philip Sheldrake has pointed out:

> Desire is at the heart of all spirituality. It is an energy that powers spirituality but, conversely, spirituality is concerned with how people focus desire. Christian spirituality embodies the sense that humanity has a longing that can only be satisfied in God. Consequently, its greatest teachers focus on how desire should be channelled.[14]

It might also be added that the sense of search, or desire, drives the conversation between belief and experience in the exploration of Christian spirituality. Or to put it another way, it is desire which leads one to knock on the door of long-held beliefs with the challenge of new experience or to tap at the gate of treasured experience with questions raised by critical study and reflection.

These three key components: (un)belief in God, desire, and the experience of relationship, form the building blocks to any approach to Christian spirituality. It is to these fundamental components that we now give attention.

Draw your own conclusions

Have you ever known anyone like the 'very religious people' encountered in the traveller's tale? Why was each approach not satisfactory? How do you understand the phrase 'I am more interested in relationship than religion'?

Examine the following definitions of Christian spirituality. Explore the focus of each definition. Do the definitions seem to concentrate on doctrine or experience? Can you identify a sense of desire in each one? How does it find expression?

Christian spirituality concerns the quest for a fulfilled and authentic Christian existence, involving the bringing together of the fundamental ideas of Christianity and the whole experience of living on the basis of and within the scope of the Christian faith.

> Alister E. McGrath (1999), *Christian Spirituality: An Introduction*, Oxford: Blackwell, p. 2.

Christian spirituality is the lived encounter with Jesus Christ in the Spirit. In that sense, Christian spirituality is concerned not so much with doctrines of Christianity as with the ways those teachings shape us as individuals who are part of the Christian community who live in the larger world.

> Lawrence S. Cunningham and Keith J. Egan (1996), *Christian Spirituality: Themes from the Tradition*, New York: Paulist Press, p. 7.

Spirituality is what 'makes us tick'. It is the sum of forces, influences, beliefs, disciplines, conscious or unconscious, which possess us, determine our motives and behaviour and shape our personalities.

> Gordon Wakefield (2001), *Groundwork of Christian Spirituality*, Peterborough: Epworth Press, p. 1.

Reflect on John O'Donohue's statement that spirituality is the 'art of transfiguration'. What do you think he means?

Sociologists point to the way culture and cultural conditioning may shape religious experience. What specific examples of this can you think of?

Think about engagement with art or music. In what way is it 'more than it is'? How might this same analogy apply to religious experience?

Why is it not satisfactory to think of spirituality in terms of doctrine or experience? Do you think that 'desire drives spirituality'?

Further reading

Introductions to Christian spirituality

Lawrence S. Cunningham and Keith J. Egan (1996), *Christian Spirituality: Themes from the Tradition*, New York: Paulist Press.

Michael Downing (1997), *Understanding Christian Spirituality*, New York: Paulist Press.

Arthur Holder (ed.) (2005), *The Blackwell Companion to Christian Spirituality*, Oxford: Blackwell.

Urban T. Holmes (1981), *A History of Christian Spirituality: An Analytical Introduction*, New York: The Seabury Press.

Bradley P. Holt (2005), *Thirsty for God: A Brief History of Christian Spirituality*, Minneapolis: Fortress Press.

Alister E. McGrath (1999), *Christian Spirituality: An Introduction*, Oxford: Blackwell.

Philip Sheldrake (ed.) (2005), *The New SCM Dictionary of Christian Spirituality*, London: SCM Press.

Gordon S. Wakefield (2001), *Groundwork of Christian Spirituality*, Peterborough: Epworth Press.

Readings on the relationship between theology and spirituality

Diogenes Allen (1977), *Spiritual Theology*, Boston, Mass.: Cowley.

Mark A. McIntosh (1998), *Mystical Theology*, Oxford: Blackwell.

Philip Sheldrake (1998), *Spirituality and Theology*, London: Darton, Longman & Todd.

Psychology and spiritual development

Christopher Bryant (1983), *Jung and the Christian Way*, London: Darton, Longman & Todd.

James W. Fowler (1981/1995), *Stages of Faith: The Psychology of Human Development and the Quest for Meaning*, San Francisco: Harper & Row.

Leslie Francis (1997), *Personality Type and Scripture: Exploring Mark's Gospel*, London: Mowbray.

Malcolm Goldsmith (1994/1997), *Knowing Me, Knowing God: Exploring Your Spirituality with Myers-Briggs*, London: SPCK.

Liberation theologies

Leonardo Boff (1997), *Cry of the Earth, Cry of the Poor*, Maryknoll, N.Y.: Orbis.

Kathleen Fischer (1989), *Women at the Well: Feminist Perspectives on Spiritual Direction*, London: SPCK.

Gustavo Gutiérrez (1984), *We Drink From Our Own Wells: The Spiritual Journey of A People*, London: SCM Press.

Elizabeth A. Johnson (2001), *She Who Is: The Mystery of God in Feminist Discourse*, New York: Crossroad Publishing.

Ursula King (1994), *Feminist Theology From the Third World: A Reader*, London: SPCK.

Catherine Mowry LaCugna (1991), *God For Us: the Trinity and Christian Life*, San Francisco: Harper.

Ann Loades (1990), *Feminist Theology, A Reader*, London: SPCK.

Fran Porter (2004), *It Will Not Be Taken Away From Her, A Feminist Engagement With Women's Christian Experience*, London: Darton, Longman & Todd.

Rosemary Radford Ruether (1983), *Sexism and God-Talk: Towards a Feminist Theology*, London: SCM Press.

Jon Sobrino (1994), *The Principle of Mercy, Taking the Crucified People from the Cross*, Maryknoll, N.Y.: Orbis.
Theo Witvliet (1985), *A Place in the Sun, An Introduction to Liberation Theology in the Third World*, London: SCM Press.

Postmodernism

Walter Truett Anderson (ed.) (1996), *The Fontana Postmodernism Reader*, London: Fontana.
Stanley J. Grenz and John R. Franke (2001), *Beyond Foundationalism: Shaping Theology in a Postmodern Context*, Louisville/London: Westminster John Knox Press.
David Harvey (1990/2000), *The Condition of Postmodernity*, Oxford: Blackwell.
Paul Lakeland (1997), *Postmodernity: Christian Identity in a Fragmented Age*, Minneapolis: Fortress Press.
Alasdair MacIntyre (1984), *After Virtue: A Study in Moral Theory*, Notre Dame, Indiana: University of Notre Dame Press.
J. Richard Middleton and Brian J. Walsh (1995), *Truth is Stranger Than It Used to Be: Biblical Faith in a Post-Modern Age*, Downers Grove, Illinois: Inter-Varsity Press.
Michael Riddell (1998), *Threshold of the Future: Reforming the Church in the Post-Christian West*, London: SPCK.
Kevin J. Vanhoozer (ed.) (2003), *The Cambridge Companion to Postmodern Theology*, Cambridge: Cambridge University Press.

Notes

1 John O'Donohue (1997), *Anam Cara*, London: Bantam Books, p. 82.

2 The phrase 'it is more than it is' is used by Rowan Williams (2005), *Grace and Necessity*, London: Continuum Books. This is perhaps a rather difficult work for those just starting out in the study of Christian faith, but it provides a challenging discussion on love, theology and art.

3 Walter Brueggemann (1984), *The Message of the Psalms*, Minneapolis: Augsburg Publishing House, pp. 21ff. introduced me to the language of 'orientation, disorientation, new orientation'.

4 Elizabeth Schüssler Fiorenza (1983), *In Memory of Her: A Feminist Theological Reconstruction of Christian Origins*, London: SCM Press. Daphne Hampson (1990), *Theology and Feminism*, Oxford: Blackwell.

5 Dorothy Day (1952), *The Long Loneliness*, New York: Harper & Row, pp. 132ff.

6 C. S. Lewis (1955), *Surprised by Joy*, Glasgow: William Collins Sons and Co., p. 179.

7 Nicola Slee (2004), *Women's Faith Development, Patterns and Processes*, Aldershot, Hants: Ashgate.

8 Jung claimed he was using the word 'spirituality' in the intellectual not the

supernatural sense. C. G. Jung (1963), *Memories, Dreams, Reflections*, New York: Vintage Books, p. 149.

9 The Myers-Briggs Type Indicator is a personality inventory based on Jung's theories of psychological types. It was developed by Katharine Cook Briggs (1875–1968), and her daughter Isabel Briggs Myers (1897–1980) who applied Jung's ideas to human interaction. For an introduction to the Myers-Briggs Indicator, see David Keirsey and Marilyn Bates (1984), *Please Understand Me*, Del Mar, CA: Prometheus Nemesis; Isabel Briggs Myers and Peter Briggs (1980), *Gifts Differing*, Palo Alto, CA: Consulting Psychologists Press.

10 Trinity as community is discussed further in Chapter 3.

11 Gordon Wakefield (1983), *Dictionary of Christian Spirituality*, London: SCM Press, p. v. James McClendon (1974/1990), *Biography as Theology*, Philadelphia: Trinity Press.

12 James Woodward and Stephen Pattison (2000), 'An Introduction to Pastoral and Practical Theology', in James Woodward and Stephen Pattison (eds), *The Blackwell Reader in Pastoral and Practical Theology*, Oxford: Blackwell, p. 7.

13 Marie McCarthy (2000), 'Spirituality in a Postmodern Era', in Woodward and Pattison, *The Blackwell Reader in Pastoral and Practical Theology*, p. 204.

14 Philip Sheldrake (2005), 'Desire' in Philip Sheldrake (ed.), *The New SCM Dictionary of Christian Spirituality*, London: SCM Press, p. 231. See also, Philip Sheldrake (1994), *Befriending Our Desires*, London: Darton, Longman & Todd.

1

Belief, Search and Relationship

On a train journey I fell into conversation with someone who had been put off the Christian faith because he pictured God as a harsh unrelenting judge. He had experienced a great deal of pain in life and someone had told him that all that had happened to him was God's judgement on him. Basically he had decided that if that is what Christian faith claims God is like, he wanted no part of it. And I could see why. In fact, I told him that if God was like that I would not believe either.

Sometimes, in the mind's eye, a person may tend to think of God as a great judge in the sky watching and waiting for one of us to do something wrong so that we may be punished severely. God is sometimes described as the benevolent king or believed by some people to be an eternal watchmaker who keeps everything in working order.[1] Since spirituality is a process of discovery and part of the ongoing transfiguration of life, it follows that every person will have a different kind of experience of God. To some people this is troubling, because the validity of personal experience is secured by identifying certain similarities with others. In this view, the assurances of faith are sought by trying to identify some particular doctrinal and/or experiential agreement.

At the beginning of the twentieth century, the American philosopher William James gave the Gifford Lectures in Edinburgh, which were later published as *The Varieties of Religious Experience* (1902). Largely ignoring institutional or ecclesiastical organization, James attempted to explore the phenomenon of personal religious experience.[2] While at times he has been criticized for putting too much emphasis on feeling at the expense of doctrinal clarity, the result was at the very least an outline of the wide *varieties* of human experience that might be counted as religious.

To claim that there are many Christian spiritualities may seem to be following a similar path to that which William James cut nearly a century ago. By speaking of many spiritualities, it perhaps appears that we are suggesting that any experience which is claimed by a Christian may be counted as part of Christian spirituality. This claim would be hotly disputed among many Christians, especially those who feel that a particular doctrine or experience is a hallmark of Christian faith. Yet, the history of the Church attests to the fact that any attempt to unite Christians along a set of doctrines or practices is highly problematic. Moreover, any attempt to identify what may be considered normative to Christian faith must first acknowledge and consider carefully the breadth of interpretation of Christian doctrine and experience.

Christian tradition affirms the belief that all human beings are made uniquely in God's image, but each has a different personality, a different background, and a different context in which we 'live and move and have our being' (Acts 17.28). While there has been some debate over whether spirituality is related more to doctrine or to experience, as I have already tried to show, the mark of authentic Christian spirituality is not to be associated with certain doctrinal formulations or experiences. Verbal agreement or mental assent to a particular set of doctrines does not make a Christian, nor does a claim to a particular experience. Yet, both what one believes to be true and what one claims to have experienced in relationship with God, others and the wider world are at the heart of the conversation that takes place as individuals give themselves to the search for meaning.

In the Introduction, I introduced three general themes or what I have called the components of Christian spirituality: belief in God, desire, and the experience of relationship. While for the purposes of discussion we shall explore each of these three components in turn, it is important to keep in mind that they are in fact intertwined and inseparable. Like a helix composed of many interwoven threads or like overlapping circles, each becomes an integral part of the other.

Belief in God: 'The beyond in our midst'[3]

Belief in God is a foundational element of Christian spirituality. However we may conceive of God, whatever our particular picture of God, however we might imagine God to be, at the very least, Christian spirituality asserts that God exists. Yet, belief in God does not presuppose that we may know God completely. It may be argued that any attempt to define or describe God should be resisted because any definition of God ultimately reflects the limitations of an individual's own experience and language. Or to put it another way, doctrine merely reflects the limits of one's experience.

Naturally, people have imagined what God is like and drawing on their own experience and from their own culture biblical writers depicted God in many different ways: as a stern judge, a victorious king, a shepherd, a warrior, a lover, etc. Biblical pictures are not to be taken as the sum total of all that we may say about God, since the language we use to speak of God is the language of comparison. It is metaphor and simile because, as Rex Mason has pointed out, 'when we speak of something beyond our present knowledge and experience, we have to start from what we do know'.[4] In the New Testament, Jesus is often portrayed as one who challenged the way people thought about God or imagined God to act. He too, according to the Gospel accounts, used simile to suggest to his followers new ways of thinking about God. The love of God is likened to a woman sweeping her house to find a lost coin and rejoicing when the coin has been found (Luke 15.8–10). God's kingdom, that is God's rule, is likened to yeast that is mixed with flour and leavens all of it, or to a tiny mustard seed which when planted grows into a large shrub (Matthew 13.31–33). All of these images are intended to take something quite ordinary, small or seemingly insignificant and point to the way it is actually much more than it appears. By using images of the ordinary, Jesus draws attention to the extraordinary love and activity of God. Moreover, the Gospel writers highlight the fact that the way the people have imagined God seemed unable to take account of his inexpressible love and forgiveness. In short, the limits of human imagination mean that any attempt to describe God results in a partial picture of God.

The pictures with which we are comfortable and the language which we think gives expression to God ultimately reflects our own experience of life, culture and the wider world. The limits of language and the barriers of culture have been highlighted by the fact that for many years a predominantly masculine and largely patriarchal culture within the Christian Church failed to take account of the inclusiveness, femininity and diversity within God.[5] The dominance of cultural values and traditions, particularly within the Christian Church in the West, has also shaped the way that many people imagine God as well as the way the Church has been perceived.

While noting the limits of language and the shaping influence of culture within the Christian tradition, there is a firm view that God is both transcendent and immanent. God is the 'beyond in our midst'.[6] The mystery of a God who is hidden and revealed, immanent and transcendent, present and yet beyond us is expressed in different ways. In the Gospel of John the proclamation is made that God has made himself known to us by making his home (literally, 'pitching his tent') among us: the 'word became flesh and lived among us'. Early Christians struggled to understand the nature of God incarnate and debated how to put into words what they had experienced and believed to be true about God. However, as they tried to explain the idea that Jesus, as God's Son, was both divine and human, they often placed more emphasis on one rather than the other or believed that to enlarge one perspective meant that the other had to be diminished. The result was that early Church councils spent countless hours arguing over whether Christ was 'equal to' and 'of one substance with' the Father and if so what that meant.[7] Later there was more discussion about how God might be understood as a Trinity or one God in three persons. Yet it would seem that people were using language to try to describe some aspect of their experience of God. However, as Paul Fiddes has pointed out, perhaps the best language to use when speaking of the Trinity is not 'observational language' ('so that is what God looks like') but 'language of participation'.[8]

The danger with all the debate over the right words to use about God is that people take their eyes off relationship with God. Out of all the doctrinal machinations that have occurred for centuries, the key point, which Christians sometimes lose sight of, is that a belief in God who is both immanent and transcendent means that relationship is possible. Our relationship with God is not of course a relationship of equals. Neither is it what the Jewish existentialist philosopher Martin Buber referred to as an 'I–It' relationship. That is to say, it is not a meeting simply with an idea or concept, an image if you like. Rather it is an 'I–Thou' (in some modern translations 'I–You') relationship which implies an encounter or meeting with another or, in the case of God, 'The Holy Other'. This 'I–You' relationship with God as Buber described it suggests that God is not merely an object of our experience or of our thought. God may not be defined and analysed, yet human beings continually desire to make God an object of faith.[9] As he put it:

> By its very nature the eternal You cannot become an It; because by its very nature it cannot be placed within measure or limit, not even within the measure of the immeasurable and the limit of the unlimited; because by its very nature it cannot be grasped as a sum of qualities, not even as an infinite sum of qualities that have been raised to transcendence; because it is not to be found either in or outside the world; because it cannot be experienced; because it cannot be thought; because we transgress against it, against that which has being, if we say: 'I believe that he is' – even 'he' is still a metaphor, while 'you' is not.[10]

At one level, Buber is focusing on the idea that relationship or encounter with the Holy Other which leads to responsible action in the world is far more important than a fact of revelation which becomes the object of devotion in and of itself. Or to put it another way, 'relationship is more than religion'.

Christians believe that the possibility of encounter and relationship with God is opened to people through the life, death and resurrection of Jesus Christ. The way people meet God and understand and practise their faith is in itself open to endless debate. When belief becomes the focus of discussion and debate, often the idea of revelation becomes more important than the encounter with the one revealed.

Yet, in Christian spirituality the important point is the claim of Christians that personal relationship is possible with God not because we know and love God (or perhaps we could say, we know about God and love the ideas about God) but because God loves us and sent Jesus, to show us how to love (1 John 4.10). Hence many Christian spiritual writers would claim that those who search for God will not 'find' God, but will perhaps be encountered by the Holy Other and in some way be found by the love of God. Thomas Kelly, an American Quaker, put it this way: 'God the initiator, God the aggressor, God the seeker, God the stirrer into life, God the ground of our obedience, God the giver of the power to become children of God.'[11]

Even while affirming that God's love has been revealed in the life, death and resurrection of Christ and that it is made known now by the presence of the Holy Spirit most Christians would recognize that there are many different ways both to understand and to experience the love of God. Where these differences appear is in the claim that resurrection faith assumes that God remains present and may be encountered in the here and now. Unfortunately, in an eagerness to highlight God's presence with us, at times some Christians have lost sight of God's transcendence. That is to say, while some Christians are quick to point out that 'God is with us', they are often less able to accept that God is, at the same time, 'beyond us'. The balance is found in a God who is in fact the 'beyond in our midst'. 'God is the "I am", existence itself, "besides whom there is no other". God encompasses the boundaries of all existence, including God's own.'[12]

The loss of emphasis on transcendence means that many Christians speak as if it is possible 'to know' God. Yet, if transcendence is taken seriously, then we must admit that human beings may never know God fully, for God is beyond all knowledge and all thought. There is a point at which language breaks down, a point beyond which it cannot go and, as we shall see, a point where experience is always limited and limiting as well. Eberhard Jüngel described a conversation he had with Martin Heidegger:

> Toward the end of his life I had a conversation with Heidegger about the relation between thought and language, and I asked whether it wasn't the destiny of thought to be on the way to God (*unterwegs zu Gott*). He answered: 'God – that is the most worthy object of thought. But that's where language breaks down.'[13]

Out of this brief discussion of God's immanence and transcendence, for our purposes here it is important to note simply that there are many different ways of knowing God. Perhaps even that there are as many ways of knowing as there are individuals. Yet clearly no such knowledge is ever complete. The paradox of Christian spirituality is that when we speak of relationship with God, it is only when we give up seeking to know God that God is encountered or known, or to put it simply: in not knowing one may know. The anonymous author of *The Cloud of Unknowing* described it in this way:

> Now you say, 'How shall I proceed to think of God as he is in himself?' To this I can only reply, 'I don't know.'
>
> With this question you bring me into the very darkness and cloud of unknowing that I want you to enter. A man [person] may know completely and ponder thoroughly every created thing and its works, yes, and God's works, too, but not God himself. Thought cannot comprehend God. And so, I prefer to abandon all I can know, choosing rather to love him whom I cannot know. Though we cannot know him we can love him. By love he may be touched and embraced, never by thought. Of course, we do well at times to ponder God's majesty or kindness for the insight these meditations may bring. But in the real contemplative work you must set all this aside and cover it over with the cloud of forgetting. Then let your loving desire, gracious and devout, step bravely and joyfully beyond it and reach out to pierce the darkness above. Yes, beat upon that thick cloud of unknowing with the dart of your loving desire and do not cease come what may.[14]

The author's emphasis on knowing by not knowing underscores the fact that the nature of God is such that one can never fully encounter all that there is to be encountered in God. There is always more to be grasped and understood. Always more to be experienced; always more to search for and long for.

Many spiritual writers across the centuries have spoken of the dangers of too quickly seeking to make God in our own image or claiming to have a certain knowledge of God's nature. Anthony Bloom (1914–2003), the archbishop of the Russian Orthodox Church in Britain from 1962 to 1974, said it is the

> living God, that every human soul from millenium to millenium is in search of – a God so different from the static images offered by the manifold, successive religions. St Gregory of Nazianzus, in the fourth century, said that when we have gathered from the Scriptures, from tradition and from the experience of the Church, all that man [human-kind] has been able to know of God, and have constructed a coherent image from it, however beautiful the image may be, we have only constructed an idol. Because, as soon as we make an image of God and say: 'Look, this is God', we transform the dynamic, living, unfathom-able, infinitely profound God who is our God, into something limited, of human dimensions . . .[15]

Bloom's comment not only suggests that humans have a tendency to create God in their own image, but likewise that their image-making is driven by some deep sense of search. It is to this idea of search that we turn next.

Searching for God

One of the most oft-quoted lines in Christian spirituality is the phrase by St Augustine, 'our heart is restless until it rests in you'.[16] For some this 'rest' implies that knowledge and experience of God may be realized in life and that the restless search of the deepest inner self may be brought to completion. Summed up in the rather crass notion that one has 'found God', the idea conveyed is that God is discovered as one would uncover treasure; once found, never lost again. The image of the discovery of treasure is, of course, found in the New Testament in the teachings of Jesus where the kingdom of God is likened to discovering treasure in a field and a pearl of great price (Matthew 13.44–46). In these parables it seems that Jesus' listeners are encouraged to 'seek and find'. Yet it is im-portant to note that these parables refer to seeking the 'kingdom of God' which is not to be equated with merely an acceptance of God's existence, as though God could be discovered rather as one finds hidden treasure. Rather 'the kingdom' seems to refer to God's rule or reign. It has more to do with seeking God's will or God's way or, perhaps better stated, giving oneself to God's sphere of activity than realizing all there is to know about God. Moreover, seeking the kingdom as it is described in the Gospels is understood as an ongoing process. 'Finding', therefore, seems to refer to discovering again and again what it means to experience God in different ways and in different situations.

The search, then, is not to be seen as a once and for all event. It is an ongoing process of growing understanding. Presumably the followers of Jesus were searching and finding and discovering and rediscovering what the love of God meant in many different ways. The search for God is not simply to be recognized and labelled with a definable end. It is ongoing, indeed, a lifelong process. As Teilhard de Chardin put it,

> God does not offer himself to our finite beings as a thing all complete and ready to be embraced. For us he is eternal discovery and eternal growth. The more we think we understand him, the more he reveals himself as otherwise. The more we think we hold him, the further he withdraws, drawing us into the depths of himself.[17]

A sense of longing, of course, is not limited to Christians. Many would argue that search, longing or desire is in some way innate to all human experience. John Macquarrie suggested that the idea of 'the quest' has been 'present in experience from the beginning'.[18] He claims that 'it belongs to the very structure of human experience'.[19] It is related to our sense of 'endings and beginnings', to our desire for belonging, to an idea of 'coming home'. The fundamental commonality of search and longing to living beings is recognized by poets and philosophers. T. S. Eliot captures the essence of longing in *Four Quartets*:

> With the drawing of this Love and the voice of this Calling
> We shall not cease from exploration . . .[20]

Whether or not one would want to claim that this sense of search is an innate human experience, like the traveller in our opening story, most people recognize the deep longing for something which has not yet been found. It is this desire that has driven explorers, motivated athletes, and pushed scientists to discover new frontiers and reach new heights. The sense of longing is what keeps a writer at his desk and a musician with her instrument.

In Christian spirituality, desire is first and foremost a desire for God. Christians identify with the words of the psalmist who exclaimed: 'as a deer longs for flowing streams, so my soul longs for you, O God' (Psalm

42.1), or with the image in the parables of Jesus of a person who is far from home and yearns to return to the parent's home. The New Testament has many stories about people who come to Jesus because they seem to be searching for something. They ask questions about life, faith, peace, healing and hope. They are all portrayed as those who are looking for something which they have not yet found. While some Christians today claim with great exuberance that 'Jesus is the answer', the New Testament witness claims that Jesus is 'the Way' which implies that, in human terms, the search is ongoing (John 14.6).

Some Christians, of course, are not content to talk about searching for God, or at least not in the sense that a search is always in progress. Many would feel far more comfortable with the biblical picture of being 'lost and found' by God. For them, one may be 'lost' for a time but once the way is discovered or one has been 'found', the search is over. Their logic goes something like this: if someone is looking for direction it is primarily because that person is lost and searching for the way. If someone seeks, eventually that person will find or be found. The biblical pictures of a lost sheep being gently brought back into the fold or the prodigal child finally returning home have been used to support this view that those who are 'lost' may be 'found' (Luke 15.1–32).

This idea of 'being found' seems to have held far more attention in popular Christian experience than the idea of our search for God or God's search for us. Yet, there is a strand of biblical teaching which points to God's longing for us. Like the father waiting for the wayward child to return home, so God longs for us to return, so that we may meet or be met by God. God is, in fact, a God of desire. The idea of God being a desiring God is important to Christian spirituality and central to our understanding of our own search. Theologians have long spoken of our capacity for relationship as an indication that we are made in God's own image, but as Philip Sheldrake has pointed out, perhaps desire too is a result of our being made in the image of God.[21] The idea of God longing for us and our longing for God is often seen in the Bible. Through the prophet Hosea, God speaks as a parent who cannot give up on her children (Hosea 11.1–9). She loves them with a longing, which will not cease to bend and stoop on their behalf. Or, in the Song of Solomon, we find the very emotive images of a lover seeking the beloved:

Upon my bed at night
I sought him whom my soul loves;
I sought him, but found him not;
I called him, but he gave no answer.

'I will rise now and go about the city,
in the streets and in the squares;
I will seek him whom my soul loves.'
I sought him, but found him not.

The sentinels found me, as they went about in the city.
'Have you seen him whom my soul loves?'
Scarcely had I passed them,
when I found him whom my soul loves.

(Song 3.1–4a)

This idea of God's desire for us and our desire for God is reflected in the words of Catherine of Siena, a fourteenth-century Christian who suggested that God needs us and wants us even as we need and want God. She explained this by saying that God, the 'mad lover', had fallen in love with his creatures. She wrote:

O eternal, infinite Good! O mad lover! And you have need of your creature? It seems so to me, for you act as if you could not live without her, in spite of the fact that you are Life itself, and everything has life from you and nothing can have life without you.

Why then are you so mad? Because you have fallen in love with what you have made! You are pleased and delighted over her within yourself, as if you were drunk for her salvation. She runs away from you and you go looking for her. She strays and you draw closer to her: You clothed yourself in our humanity, and nearer than that you could not have come.[22]

Likewise, the poem *The Hound of Heaven* by Francis Thompson seems to describe the idea of the search as a double search; God is searching for us even as we are searching for God. God is the 'hound of heaven baying at our heels'. Thompson wrote:

I fled Him, down the nights and down the days;
I fled Him, down the arches of the years;
I fled Him, down the labyrinthine ways
Of my own mind; and in the mist of tears
I hid from Him, and under running laughter.
     Up vistaed hopes I sped;
     And shot, precipitated,

Adown Titanic glooms of chasmèd fears,
From those strong Feet that followed, followed after
    But with unhurrying chase,
    And unperturbèd pace,
Deliberate speed, majestic instancy,
    They beat – and a Voice beat
    More instant than the Feet –
'All things betray thee, who betrayest Me.'[23]

The idea of searching or longing relates closely to the idea of journey or pilgrimage in the Christian tradition. Before they were called Christians, members of the early Church were known as followers of the Way. From the beginning, Christian writers depicted faith as a willingness to set off on a journey much like Abraham and Sarah had left home without knowing where they were going; 'faith is the assurance of things hoped for, the conviction of things unseen' (Hebrews 11.1). This idea of longing or desire combined with a sense of journey is depicted in a prayer by the twentieth-century writer and monk, Thomas Merton:

My Lord God,
I have no idea where I am going.
I do not see the road ahead of me.
I cannot know for certain where it will end.
Nor do I really know myself, and the fact
that I think I am following your will
does not mean that I am actually doing so.
But I believe that the desire to please you
does in fact please you. And I hope I have
that desire in all that I am doing.
I hope that I will never do anything apart
from that desire. And I know that if I do
this you will lead me by the right road,
though I may know nothing about it.
Therefore I will trust you always though
I may seem to be lost and in the shadow of death.
I will not fear, for you are ever with me, and you
will never leave me to face my perils alone.[24]

Merton's description of an ongoing search for God who cannot be fully and completely described or understood is at the heart of Christian spirituality. The search will not lead simply to Scripture or tradition for an answer. As we have already noted, God is not to be contained by the language of sacred text or in creed or confessional statements. God will not be boxed in by individual perspective or limited to tradition or merely reflect cultural experience. That is not to say that the broader historical tradition of Christian faith is not important. The search for God as understood by Christians may lead through the Scripture and tradition, but it will not be limited by them.

Of course, Christian spirituality should not be seen as an individual search for truth or a lone journey to God. Rather there is a very real sense in which the search for God and God's search for humankind takes place within a corporate context. Many Christians have struggled to hold fast to the idea of individual freedom to search for God alongside the idea that the search takes place within a commitment to others as part of the body of Christ. In particular, Christians have struggled with how the sense of an individual's ongoing search for God's way may be carried out if they are part of a larger corporate body which demands allegiance to particular interpretations of Scripture and expressions of Christian doctrine. In short, if individuals continue to search and bring questions to faith, how might that be done while still walking with others who claim that their questions have already been answered by a particular reading of the Bible? The response is surely that any search demands the recognition, as one seventeenth-century Christian put it, that there is 'yet more light and truth to break forth from the Word'.[25] That is to say that the Bible, as a guide for Christian faith and practice, is open to a variety of interpretations. This is what Thomas Merton meant when he wrote:

> To accept the Bible in its wholeness is not easy. We are much more inclined to narrow it down to a one-track interpretation which actually embraces only a very limited aspect of it. And we dignify that one-track view with the term 'faith'. Actually it is the opposite of faith: it is an escape from the mature responsibility of faith which plunges into the many-dimensional, the paradoxical, the conflicting elements of the Bible as well as those of life itself, and finds unity not by excluding all it does not understand but by embracing and accepting things in their often disconcerting reality. We must not therefore open the Bible with any set determination to reduce it to the limits of a preconceived pattern of our own. And in reading it we must not succumb to the temptation of short-cuts and half-truths. All attempts to narrow the Bible down until it fits conveniently into the slots prepared for it by our prejudice will end with our misunderstanding the Bible and even falsifying its truth.[26]

Merton was correct. Christian history, however, points to many examples of those who insisted on pre-ordaining the limits of the search for truth. Yet, the many approaches to Christian spirituality affirm that the long-ing for truth, which is God, not only leads us into a deeper engagement with Scripture, but into a deeper experience of relationship with God. It is to this final facet of spirituality, namely relationship, that we now give attention.

Loving God and loving people: the experience of relationship

As we have already seen, at times there have been those within the Church who have divided belief from action and separated doctrine from experi-ence. When that happens, it becomes possible to begin to think of faith and spirituality primarily as adherence to correct doctrine or worship on the one hand, or simply doing good deeds on the other. Yet, as we have noted, Christian spirituality is not merely believing particular doctrines of faith. Nor is it to be evaluated according to worship attendance or style, nor is it judged by ethical action alone. Christian spirituality may be reflected in lifestyle and action, but it should not be evaluated on those terms alone. A Christian is not Christian because he or she does good deeds. Nor is a Christian to be counted Christian because she goes to church often or prays publicly. Rather Christian spirituality is shaped by both action and contemplation and expressed in both word and deed. Driven by the desire to know and to be known by God, Christian spir-ituality develops as beliefs are examined in the light of experience of relationship with God, others and the wider world and vice versa.

Christian faith is founded on a relationship with God through Jesus Christ. Indeed, Christians believe that it is this relationship which shapes all other relationships that one may have with others or with the wider world. The relationship that one may have with God in Christ will be unique to the individual. No relationship will be identical to another relationship. Of course, just as we may recognize similarities in our ex-perience of human relationships with parents or siblings, neighbours, or friends, so Christians speak of recognizable features in their experiences of relationship with God. Yet, at the same time, it is understood that no one relationship between an individual and God in Christ will be identi-cal to the relationship of another. This sense of individuality and unique-ness of relationship is one reason, perhaps the primary reason, why there is not one Christian spirituality but many spiritualities. Hence, although Christians sometimes try to limit Christian faith to one set of beliefs or

33

doctrines, in fact, relationship with God can never be reduced to a simple set of ideas, rules or regulations. Rather the Christian way is about love, love known in relationship with God and with others.

The emphasis on love for God and love for others as the basis for the Christian way is made plain by a story in the New Testament: a man who came to Jesus and asked 'what must I do to inherit eternal life?' Jesus responded by asking 'What is written in the law? What do you read there?' It is reported that the man replied: 'You shall love the Lord your God with all your heart, and with all your soul, and with all your strength, and with all your mind; and your neighbour as yourself.' Jesus said to him, 'You have given the right answer; do this, and you will live' (Luke 10.25–28).

The man was not given a doctrine to believe. He was not told that his sense of longing would cease. Rather he was urged to focus his desire on love for God and love for others. Loving God and loving others: this is the essence of Christian faith and indeed at the heart of Christian spirituality. The way one gives expression to love for God and love for others results in a variety of spiritualities, as many spiritualities as there are shades of colour or varieties of song. For some this emphasis on love may seem rather wishy-washy and lacking in sound theological foundation. Yet, the emphasis on love at the heart of spirituality is not an attempt to reduce spirituality to mere sentimentality or emotion. It is not an attempt to deny the need to give expression to faith through doctrinal statement or liturgical phrase or movement. Rather it is to recognize the biblical teaching that the very nature of God is love, a love that is never reduced to a nice warm feeling, but is expressed in relationship through creative, suffering, liberating and sustaining power. Christian faith teaches that this love has been revealed by God through the life, death and resurrection of Jesus Christ. Yet the ways by which individuals discover that love and give expression to it in their own lives are too numerous to count. Hence, the profusion of Christian spiritualities.

Perhaps because people prefer clear boundaries and feel uneasy with a rather vague and seemingly simple notion that Christian faith is about love, from the very beginning there have been many attempts to define the limits of love. According to Luke's Gospel, after the man told Jesus that the two great commandments were about loving God and loving people, he sought further clarification as to who his neighbour might be. The Gospel writer claims that Jesus responded by telling a story about someone who was wounded and left by the roadside to die. In the story, it is the most unlikely person, a Samaritan (an enemy of the Jews), who demonstrated love for a wounded Jew. No explanation is given as to how this could be so; all who heard the story were told simply to 'go and do likewise' (Luke 10.29–37). The message of Jesus throughout the New Testament is that love knows no boundaries or limits.

Christian writers have reflected deeply on this and readily acknowledged that what they expressed was only a partial understanding of this way of love. In trying to probe the depths of his desire for God, Richard Rolle, a fourteenth-century English mystic, claimed that his 'whole heart, fixed in desire for Jesus, is transformed into the fire of love . . .'[27] Yet, while delighting in the gift of God's love, Rolle is keen to point out that it was impossible to fully comprehend the Giver. Rather, one experiences the inextinguishable fire which is ignited by love, and calls the individual into service for Christ.

> For the God of infinite magnitude, of inconceivable goodness, and of unspeakable sweetness which is incomprehensible to any creature, can, thus, never be comprehended by us as He exists eternally within Himself. But when the spirit has already begun to burn with desire for the Creator, it is given a capacity for uncreated light. And then, inspired and filled with the gifts of the Holy Spirit, it rejoices with such joy as is allowable to mortals, and, transcending all visible things, it is raised up to the sweetness of eternal life. And when, by the sweetness of the Godhead and the heat of Creating Light, it is poured out in a holocaust to the eternal King, offered and accepted, it is wholly consumed.
>
> O delightful Love, strong, seizing, burning, spontaneous, powerful, inextinguishable! You bring the whole soul into Your service and do not permit it to think of anything beyond You! You claim for Yourself all that we live, all that we savor, all that we are![28]

Rolle's experience of God's love which burns and glows until it flares up in outward service is not, of course, the only way to describe an experience of love. Sometimes, people have described the experience of love as a gentle tug or a beckoning call. In writing of God's love in this way, Rolle was not suggesting that there is only one way of encountering God in Christian faith. Rather, he was describing his own experience of the love of God in relationship and encouraging others to embrace or be embraced by God's love as well.

It is true, of course, that there have been Christians who have felt that the love of God needed to be codified or at least expressed in such a way that it could be easily expressed. This desire for clarity of doctrine was not out of a denial of the basic intention of love at the heart of Christian faith, rather in the beginning creeds were used to teach, define, and

summarize Christian faith. In fact, attempts to formulate Christian belief in ways that others could easily understand were, of course, also used
to refute what was widely believed to be error. Or to put it another way,
creeds were used to remind others that not everything that was being said
by people who claimed to be Christian actually expressed the Christian
way of love. Unfortunately, as it developed, doctrinal expression was not
simply a matter of trying to give expression to love. Rather, defining belief
became the means of identifying and often excluding certain individuals
or groups; it became a tool of socialization and eventually was sometimes
used as the basis for claims of power and a means of institutional control.
One need only look at the history of the inquisitions by the Church which
was a tool used to root out heresy or note the churches involvement in
apartheid in South Africa to realize that this is true.

The attempts to define 'right' belief (orthodoxy) and 'right' experience
(orthopraxy) have caused many divisions among Christian believers.
Wars have been fought, and martyrs made, over the desire to establish
one particular understanding of Christian faith. Today, while some
Christians still want to speak of doctrinal fundamentals of the faith,
many Christians could not imagine uniformity in worship styles or doctrinal expression. With increasing ecumenical and inter-faith dialogue,
there is an ever increasing appreciation of a variety of ways of knowing
and loving God and others.

Indeed, many Christians would claim that the experience of relationship is not limited to a particular kind of 'religious experience'. In fact,
one might argue that God may be known through any experience and
indeed that there may be a religious dimension to every experience if it
is part of the search to discover the way of love. Varieties of religious experience are only discovered, however, as we share our stories and listen
to the stories of others.

Draw your own conclusions

Think about the images of God which seem dominant to you and in your
own experience. How do you imagine God?

Reflect on some of the images of God that are held by other people.
How do you think a person's picture of God shapes his/her religious
experience?

Think of how different cultures shape and influence the way we imagine
God. What particular images of God might be found in India or Africa
as opposed to Britain or the USA?

Consider the way that language and culture may limit our reflection on God.

Reflect on the tension between doctrine and experience in Christian faith. Which do you think is more important: what a person knows about faith or what is experienced? By what criteria are these evaluated?

It might be said that any form of religious fundamentalism limits the search for love. Do you think this is true? Why or why not?

Think about the many varieties of Christian faith. What are some of the differences in their expression of doctrine and experience?

What difference might it make to use the language of participation rather than the language of observation when talking about God?

Further reading

Readings on spirituality

Louis Bouyer et al. (1963–1969), *A History of Christian Spirituality*, 3 vols, New York: Seabury.

Christian Spirituality (1986–1991), vols I, II, III, *World Spirituality* vols 16, 17, 18, Ewert Cousins (gen. ed.), New York: Crossroad.

Cheslyn Jones, Geoffrey Wainwright, Edward Yarnold, S.J. (eds) (1986), *The Study of Spirituality*, Oxford: Oxford University Press.

Spiritus, A Journal of Christian Spirituality, Baltimore, Maryland: Johns Hopkins University Press.

Development of doctrine and devotion in the early Church

Henry Bettenson (ed.) (1957/1982), *The Early Christian Fathers*, Oxford: Oxford University Press.

Henry Chadwick (1993, 2005), *The Early Church*, London: Penguin Books.

David L. Edwards (1997), *Christianity: The First Two Thousand Years*, London: Cassell.

William H. C. Frend (1984), *The Rise of Christianity*, Atlanta: Fortress Press.

Stuart G. Hall (1991), *Doctrine and Practice in the Early Church*, London: SPCK.

Adrian Hastings (ed.) (1999), *A World History of Christianity*, London: Cassell.

Paul Johnson (1976), *A History of Christianity*, London: Pelican.

J. N. D. Kelly (1950), *Early Christian Creeds*, London: Longmans, Green and Co.

Diarmaid MacCulloch (1987), *Groundwork of Christian History*, London: Epworth.

Christopher C. Rowland (1983), *Christian Origins*, London: SPCK.

Frances M. Young (1982), *From Nicaea to Chalcedon*, London: SCM Press.

Frances M. Young (1991), *The Making of the Creeds*, London: SCM Press.

Notes

1 This picture of God as a watchmaker is most often associated with William Paley (1802), *Natural Theology: or, Evidence of the Existence and Attributes of the Deity, collected from the appearances of nature*, edited with an introduction by Matthew D. Eddy and David Knight (2006), Oxford: Oxford University Press.

2 Stanley Hauerwas has pointed out that James never claimed to believe in the existence of God, but tried to explain the human need for experience. Stanley Hauerwas (2001/2002), *With the Grain of the Universe*, London: SCM Press, pp. 43ff.

3 This phrase is borrowed from Dietrich Bonhoeffer (1953), Letter to a Friend, 30 April 1944, in *Letters and Papers From Prison*, London: SCM Press, p. 93.

4 Rex Mason (1993), *Old Testament Pictures of God*, Oxford: Regent's Park College, p. 3.

5 For a good discussion of some of the issues relating to liberation theologies, see Catherine Mowry LaCugna (1991), *God For Us: The Trinity and Christian Life*, New York: HarperCollins, pp. 266ff.

6 Bonhoeffer says that 'the "beyond" of God is not the beyond of our perceptive faculties . . . God is the "beyond" in the midst of life'. 'The Church stands not where human powers give out, on the borders, but in the centre of the village.' Bonhoeffer, *Letters and Papers*, p. 93.

7 This famous debate was held at Nicaea in AD 325. A general introduction to some of the debates over the nature of God in the early Church may be found in W. H. C. Frend (1991), *The Early Church: From the Beginnings to 461*, London: SCM Press.

8 Paul S. Fiddes (2000), *Participating in God*, London: Darton, Longman & Todd, p. 33.

9 Martin Buber (1937/1970), *I and Thou*, tr. Walter Kaufmann, Edinburgh: T&T Clark, p. 162.

10 Buber, *I and Thou*, pp. 160–1.

11 Thomas Kelly (1947), *A Testament of Devotion*, New York: Harper & Row, p. 52.

12 E. Glenn Hinson (1995), *A Serious Call to a Contemplative Lifestyle*, revised edn, Macon, Georgia: Smyth & Helwys Publishing, p. 23.

13 Eberhard Jüngel, 'Toward the Heart of the Matter', in *Christian Century*, tr. Paul E. Capetz, 15 July 1990. This article is one in a series from the *Christian Century* magazine: 'How My Mind Has Changed'. The article was prepared for Religion Online by Ted and Winnie Brock. Accessed at www.religion-online.org on 26 April 2006.

14 *Cloud of Unknowing* (1973), ed. William Johnston, London: Image/Doubleday, pp. 54–5.

15 Anthony Bloom (1972), *Meditations on a Theme: A Spiritual Journey*, London: Mowbray, pp. 70–1.

16 St Augustine, *The Confessions of St Augustine*, tr. with introduction by John K. Ryan (1960), New York: Image/Doubleday, p. 43.

17 Pierre Teilhard de Chardin (1960), *The Divine Milieu*, New York: Harper & Row, p. 139.

18 John Macquarrie (1966, 1977), *Principles of Christian Theology*, 2nd edn, London: SCM Press, p. 6.

19 Macquarrie, *Principles*, p. 6.

20 T. S. Eliot (1944), 'Little Gidding' in *Four Quartets*, London: Faber & Faber, p. 48.

21 Philip Sheldrake (1994), *Befriending Our Desires*, London: Darton, Longman & Todd, pp. 19–35.

22 Catherine of Siena, *The Dialogue of the Seraphic Virgin*, dictated by her, while in a state of ecstasy, to her secretaries, and completed in the year of Our Lord 1370. Together with an account of her death by an eye-witness; translated from the original Italian, and preceded by an introduction on the life and times of the saint, by Algar Thorold. A new and abridged edn Westminster, Md., The Newman bookshop (1943), p. 325, cited from http://home.infionline.net/~ddisse/siena.html#anchor338759, accessed 5 May 2006.

23 Francis Thompson, 'The Hound of Heaven' found at http://www.mcs.drexel.edu/~gbrandal/Illum_html/hound.html, accessed 4 May 2006.

24 Thomas Merton (1956, 1975), *Thoughts in Solitude,* Tunbridge Wells, Burns & Oates, p. 81.

25 John Robinson was a seventeenth-century English Dissenter associated with the so-called 'Pilgrim Fathers' who sailed on the *Mayflower* from Holland and England and established the colony of Plymouth Massachusetts in 1620. While Robinson stayed behind and did not travel on the *Mayflower*, he supported their efforts. F. L. Cross and E. A. Livingstone (eds) (1978), *Oxford Dictionary of the Christian Church*, Oxford: Oxford University Press, p. 1191.

26 Thomas Merton (1972), *Opening the Bible*, London: George Allen & Unwin, pp. 58–9.

27 Richard Rolle, *The Fire of Love and The Mending of Life*, tr. with introduction by M. L. del Mastro (1981), New York: Image/Doubleday, p. 81.

28 Rolle, *Fire of Love*, p. 83.

2

A Story-formed Faith

A few years ago, a television series presented the stories of people who had been adopted as children and later were able to trace and make contact with members of their birth family. In one instance, a man, who later became a Christian pastor, told how at 19 years of age he discovered that he had been adopted. However, as he began to look for his family of origin, to his surprise, he could find no birth certificate. There was no record of his birth! As he searched to find some link with his past, he described how he felt that he had no identity, no real sense of belonging and no story to tell.[1]

The desire to know stories of the past in order to give meaning to life in the present is a shared human experience. We organize our lives by means of narrative. Stories enable us to give meaning and purpose to human experience. The lack of a story to tell can be devastating to a person's sense of self-worth. Those who have no tale of the past may feel as if they have no true identity.

Most cultures are built around shared stories which convey meaning and suggest different ways of thinking about events or solving problems, as well as offering a sense of purpose and hope. Different kinds of community form around shared story as well. For example, the now commonly practised experience of group therapy is based on the realization that hearing the stories of others, and having your own story heard, is often an important step toward well-being. Alcoholics Anonymous, the Samaritan Helpline, grief-support groups, and marriage-enrichment courses are all examples of the way that storytelling is used in groups and with individuals to move toward healing, wholeness and provide a place of belonging as well. Moreover, corporate business-management has now adopted storytelling as a way of building company loyalty, developing leaders, and bringing about change. Those who promote the idea of story in management claim that businesses and organizations are about people, not machines and the way people naturally communicate and perhaps can best grapple with what may appear to be complex ideas and changing management structure is through story.[2] Storytelling has also found a new emphasis in schools and teachers are urged to rediscover the art of telling a story, in order to communicate to children in a way that will enable them to remember. The increase in the number of websites, festivals and cultural events dedicated to storytelling also points to a revived attraction to narrative.[3]

All the attention given to storytelling in the last few years serves as a reminder of the fact that story is central to how human beings relate to one another. Narrative provides a means for interacting with one another and gives opportunity for tears or laughter and, perhaps most importantly, offers a perspective or a place to stand when trying to interpret one's own life experience. It also provides a medium for sharing and exploring Christian spirituality. Storytelling is an integral part of Christian experience. Much of what we learn about God's love and faithfulness is conveyed through stories in the Bible. But it is also true that the life stories of other people – their struggles, hopes, and dreams as well as their sorrow, mistakes and pain – enable us to discover more about relationship with God and others.

Story and the link to the past

Stories not only give individuals and communities a sense of personal identity, but also they make groups aware of their distinctiveness. The history of various groups and cultures has been handed down from generation to generation through story. These stories often become enshrined in national holidays. For instance, every year on 1 March, the Welsh tell stories of St David, the patron saint of Wales. For Americans, the last Thursday of November is a time to celebrate Thanksgiving. This is a celebration of the story of the Pilgrim fathers and mothers who themselves rejoiced with a feast after surviving a very difficult winter in the new colony they had established. The English light bonfires and set off fireworks on 5 November and recall the failed attempt by Guy Fawkes to blow up the Houses of Parliament with the king inside! And so it goes. Every culture has stories which enable them to preserve in memory some event of the past. Some stories, of course, are considered more important than others and some are remembered more readily than others. Not everyone who buys fireworks for 5 November actually remembers the story of Guy Fawkes! Yet, the existence of the story behind the holiday suggests that narrative provides the threads which weave the pattern of life or at least help people to make sense of the diverse and assorted tapestries of human existence.

Stories from the past are more than excuses for holidays, of course. They unite people in a common heritage. For people who have been driven off their land and have migrated (or been relocated) to other places, stories of their homeland and their ancestors gives a sense of belonging, or at least a feeling of alliance with others.[4] Even for those who are within a culture, but feel disenfranchised, shared story provides an opportunity to discover their uniqueness. This explains, for instance, why Alex Haley's best-selling book on the history of African-American people was called *Roots*. It likewise indicates why women have welcomed the publication of the stories of *Significant Sisters* which have sometimes been lost among the tales of 'good men' in the history books.[5] To have a story is to have a history, an identity, and may be a step toward the discovery of real kinship and community with others.

Often stories are painful, at times they are memories we would prefer to forget. For nations, local communities and individuals there are those things which give us no cause for boasting. And yet at some level, there is the deep realization that stories, even the embarrassing or heartbreaking ones, serve to remind us of where we have been and may have something to teach us as we find our way into a new future. While as individuals or groups, we may find it painful to recall certain stories from the past, history should not be told in ways that attempt to sanitize the memory of bygone days. Telling the stories may open the door to healing and wholeness. An important part of Christian faith is the belief that to admit to what has been, or even what we have been or have done or failed to do, is the first step of repentance and the desire to turn around and discover a new existence in Christ. Dark stories of anguish may spark a new awareness, a new sensitivity to the wounds and scars others bear. To hear stories of the distress and agony of the past also serves as a reminder of attitudes and actions which must never be tolerated or allowed to flourish in the world.

Several years ago, one warm, bright July afternoon I went with a group of friends to Terezín, a town about an hour by bus (60 km) from Prague. I had been told it was well worth a visit, but was unprepared for what I discovered. The town had been used as a detention centre for Jews during World War Two. Here thousands of men, women and children had been kept in intolerable conditions, many until they were transported by train to Nazi death camps. Moreover, the Nazis made propaganda films here, forcing the people to be filmed as if they were enjoying life, and doing things like watching a football match, or buying clothes in well-stocked shops. The Nazis tried to portray it as a model camp, but this was only a charade. The people were forced to exist in close, cramped conditions and treated with contempt. They were herded together like animals. The people who could have expressed the story of struggle were silenced: poets, musicians and scientists were murdered. Children were born and brought up in the misery of despair; less than one in ten of the Jews sent there survived.

Visitors to the town today may go and see where the people lived and listen to accounts of the pain and suffering of many thousands of people. As I walked around the town, it seemed that there was an atmosphere of sadness hanging over the place like a dark shadow that would never leave. In fact, it appeared that the town exists now simply to tell the story – a painful, terrible story of indignity and human suffering. Terezín's story must be told and heard. But the telling of the story, as well as the hearing of it, is a painful reminder of the past.[6]

Individually and collectively human beings need to tell and hear stories of sorrow and joy, pain and delight, success and failure. For story has the power to shape lives and mould societies. Stories rebuke and inspire, they challenge and question, they bring us to our knees in laughter and make us hide our faces in disgrace. Whether it is a story of endurance, conquest, shame or failure, stories link together past, present and future and serve as a reminder that we live in the narrative of existence.[7]

Story and the uncompleted present

Story not only provides a link to the past, but also may shape our day to day lives. Children learn by story. From a very young age they enjoy not only hearing stories of the past, but also telling stories about their present experience. Sometimes this takes the form of make-believe tales and imaginary friends. But they also need a present story in order to discover their uniqueness as individuals and find a place of belonging. As individuals, stories help provide us with a sense of self. In part, we learn family values and gain a sense of distinctiveness as parents and grandparents tell us stories from their own childhood. They also repeat stories they have heard told and in so doing they establish a sense of what it means to belong to a particular family or culture. Stories help us to re-late our heritage to the present, culturally and in a familial and personal sense, and they are often used to instil values.

As well as extending a sense of personal or familial values, one of the most important functions of story is to bind members of a community to-gether. Storytellers have played and continue to play an important role in community life. Whether it is simply providing examples of courage and hope, or challenging ethical codes or old patterns of prejudice, stories may provide people with an awareness of both the good and the disturbing aspects of community life.

Since ancient times, stories have provided a way to remind communities of people about certain customs, traditions, and values which the community have cherished. Negatively, story has also been used to offend, humiliate, and perpetuate prejudice. In the modern era, at times they have become a means of self-indulgence and attention seeking. The media often convey to us stories that are little more than idle gossip and prurient tittle-tattle having no real meaning or purpose apart from supposedly shocking the listener.

While to a certain degree, television, videos, DVDs, and other forms of visual and electronic media are used to convey a narrative experience of life, the oral tradition of storytelling may be receding from our Western day-to-day encounters. Given the fast pace of modern culture it may be that often there is simply not the space or time for a story to be told or heard. Many people may be in a work environment which allows little time for sharing stories. It is possible, in fact, to go by car into your place of employment, work in isolation most of the day (sometimes even communicating by email with someone at the next desk or in the next office), with little opportunity for personal contact, before getting in the car to drive back home where many people live alone. While businesses are beginning to realize the power of story for corporate management, often there is little time in the modern workplace for sharing personal stories. At home, personal routine or family schedules and the dependence on microwaves and fast convenience foods means that meal times are often no longer family gatherings where stories of the day may be told.

Those who have grown accustomed to life which depends on instant communication through email and text messaging and relaxation which is provided by sitting without conversation in front of the television may not realize that story requires time and space. When a story is told, attention must be given to the cadence and rhythm of the words. Notice must be taken of the pause which is silent with meaning, if the sighs of the heart are to be heard.

Douglas Steere, an American Quaker, wrote an essay entitled *On Listening To Another* which begins with a story taken from the *Journal of John Woolman*. The story is about a meeting which took place in a Native American village along the upper Susquehanna River in Pennsylvania. Woolman, an eighteenth-century Quaker, rose to speak and the interpreter who was supposed to translate Woolman's words into the native language of the people was asked to sit down and let Woolman's words go untranslated. After the meeting, the Native American chief, Papunchang, approached Woolman and through the interpreter explained that he had not understood the English words, but he said, 'I love to feel where the words come from.'[8]

This ability to listen behind and beyond the actual words which are spoken is an important part of storytelling and Christian faith. Yet, to have the ability to listen this way takes time. Steere suggests, in fact, that a true listener must have four characteristics: vulnerability, acceptance, expectancy and constancy.

Vulnerability on the part of the listener means that in some way he or she is open to being changed by what is heard. The story that is being told must matter to the listener. One cannot be detached and really listen. The second characteristic according to Steere is acceptance. By this he means that the listener does not have a hidden agenda, nor has one formed an opinion about the person or the story being told. True listening never allows a mere shrug of the shoulders nor a quick nod of the head as if the listener fully understands all that is being said. There is always the possibility that there is more to the story than the words imply, if only we are able to 'feel where the words come from'.

In addition to vulnerability and acceptance, the other characteristics of a good listener, according to Steere, are expectancy and constancy, which in many ways seem to go hand in hand. Steere claims that to listen with expectancy means that one recognizes what he calls the 'partially concealed capacities' in another person, and therefore listens in such a way that these are evoked within the speaker.[9] It is to hear and feel beyond the words and to recognize something of the possibility and potential in another which may be drawn out. But to listen in this way takes time and requires, according to Steere, great constancy on the part of the listener. Steere suggests that 'to listen another's soul into a condition of disclosure and discovery may be almost the greatest service that any human being performs for another'.[10] Indeed, one might argue that for both the speaker and the listener, there is the opportunity for a real exchange, a 'giving and receiving' which may call both parties into a new way of being. In the sharing of a story and in the knowledge that it is being heard as well as in the listening and receiving, there is an opportunity to create a place of belonging. In many ways, it would seem that the need to tell a story is matched only by the need for someone who is willing to listen.

Not every story is of equal value to another story, of course, and all aspects of a story are not as important as others. For instance, if I were to recount to you a day when I went to Oxford on a train to work in a library, the story seems to have no real significance. You might simply nod your head or perhaps before I had finished my story you might begin to tell me about a journey you made by train. However, if you were willing to listen, and I sensed that you were listening with openness, acceptance and expectancy, I might have the courage to tell you about a particular experience I had as I made the journey home.

Perhaps it would take a few minutes for me to find the words and if you listened carefully you might even hear my voice tremble and crack as I recalled the day I met a man by the name of George Armstrong. But if you were constant in your listening, the story might emerge: an encounter with a stranger which exposed my arrogance, pride and self-sufficiency. You would have to listen patiently and with expectancy of course, because to this day, when I tell the story of that chance meeting, my throat tightens and my voice quavers. I want to weep. Perhaps if you hear behind the words, if you sense where the words come from, we can share for a moment a sacred space, for stories sometimes call us to stand on holy ground.

Story has power not only to evoke memory, to unite, to give identity and purpose, but it may also have the power to call us to a different way of being. When we least expect it, we may find story breaking into the mundane and ordinary: to shape, to cleanse, to heal and to transform. Stories help us make sense out of life. They help us to shape our understanding of what is and what is not. They enable us to become. They speak to us of what we are and are not yet and in this way, they serve to remind us of an uncompleted present.

Storytelling and the Bible

In the Judaeo-Christian tradition, narrative has always been an important part of communicating the nature of faith and the faithfulness of God. In the book of Deuteronomy the people of old were urged to remember the words that they were being commanded. 'Recite them to your children and talk about them when you are at home and when you are away, when you lie down and when you rise' (Deuteronomy 6.7). They were also urged to 'remember the days of old' (32.7). Jewish religious practice captures this sense of remembering God's mercy and gracious love toward Israel, especially in ritual like the Jewish Seder, a service which retells the biblical story of the exodus.

Remembering story is vital to the Christian tradition as well. At Christmas and Easter in particular, the story is told of Jesus' birth, death and resurrection. But it is also true that every time the Bible is read or the Eucharist celebrated, most Christians believe that there is the opportunity to listen again to the stories of God's love in order to discern meaning for their lives afresh. Our differing life experiences will mean that the stories may reveal different things to us at different times. In recent years, there has been a great deal of discussion in the Christian Church about how to approach the Bible in a way that demonstrates that the listeners have 'ears to hear' (Luke 14.35) and hearts which are open to God. One approach is for the reader to engage in dialogue with the text in such a deep way that the story that is heard by the reader is obviously shaped by the reader's experience as well as the text itself. This 'reader-response' approach takes seriously the biblical claim that we must have ears to hear in order to know 'what the Spirit may be saying' at a particular time and in a particular place.[11] Clearly, listening to the Holy Other is not completely unlike listening to another. Here, too, one must listen with vulnerability, acceptance, expectancy and constancy in order to understand the story of God's love for human beings, and indeed all creation, afresh.

At times, perhaps when a story is very familiar, it is possible never fully to engage in hearing the story. Hence as the children come out dressed in shepherds' costumes and gather around a very tentative Mary and Joseph, for yet another Christmas nativity play, one may be nodding in agreement or simply thinking about what to have for tea that evening. Yet, in spite of the fact that the story has been told and retold, Christians believe that the strength of the story means that there is still the possibility of encounter with God through it. The challenge to the listener is to be open and constant, vulnerable and most of all expecting that the story has the power to convey something to us or indeed within us. The danger, of course, is that people stop listening because we believe we know the stories and, indeed, we assume we know the meaning of them for us. In the context of Christian spirituality, this kind of flat approach to Scripture may be a way of avoiding encounter with God through Scripture and it seems to deny the power of story to speak and go on speaking into every age and situation.

Jesus recognized the strength of formal storytelling within a community as an act of remembering God's love and faithfulness. Hence, he observed the Jewish festivals and feasts which were organized around the narrative of God's dealings with his people in the past. Yet in addition to formal experiences of storytelling in worship, he likewise found time to stop and listen to the stories of others. As he listened, he evoked the power of the story to challenge, to rebuke, and to inspire the one who was speaking. He had the ability to hear where the words came from and replied in a way that went to the heart of the matter. Quite often he responded to people with a story. That is to say, he spoke in parables which called upon the listeners to hear beyond the words – to recognize the real issues at stake which were often not immediately obvious.

For instance, on one occasion, we are told that someone in the crowd said to Jesus, 'Teacher, tell my brother to divide the family inheritance with me.' Then warning them against thinking that life consists of the 'abundance of possessions', Jesus told a story about a rich man who filled his barns and then, when he had more than he could put in them, decided to pull down the barns and build bigger ones to store his grain and his goods, thinking that then he could say to his soul, 'Soul, you have ample goods laid up for many years, relax, eat, drink, be merry.' But God said to him, 'You fool! This very night your life is being demanded of you. And the things you have prepared whose will they be?' (Luke 12.13–21).

The story is intended to be more than a story about the just settlement of property. If one listens beyond the story, it is possible among other things to hear a message about greed, self-centredness, stewardship of time and lack of relationship with God and others. There are no doubt many other messages conveyed through that one story. The parables allowed Jesus to speak about God and God's love in ways that both challenged the listeners on many different levels and called them to a new way of being. Later, when the stories were recalled by the Gospel writers, the parables were a reminder to their Christian communities and to subsequent generations of Christians of certain aspects of devotion and commitment that are deemed important to Christian faith.

As we hear the stories, however, time and time again we are reminded of the need to listen in order to 'hear where the words come from'. The meaning of Scripture is not found in an easy translation of words. Jesus claimed that to speak in parables is a reminder of the hidden things which for some 'seeing they do not perceive, and hearing they do not listen, nor do they understand' (Matthew 13.10–15; Mark 4.10–12; Luke 8.9–10). Perhaps part of what we are to comprehend here is that there is always more to be understood about God's love and grace. These texts are warnings against a mere cursory reading of Scripture and an easy nod of the head which implies that we understand.

Bible stories are not intended simply to record past events. They are not to be read and recalled simply as literal historical accounts. Rather they are stories which continue to speak to the present and shape the future. Of course the stories at times do call the hearer to remember the past; Christians reflect on God's faithfulness in days gone by, but stories also call us to examine the present. The stories in fact have power to shape the present and call us into a different future. These are stories which may speak individually or collectively of sin and failure. Jesus and the Gospel writers who repeated them after him used the stories to challenge and rebuke as well as encourage and transform. Those who listen carefully know that the stories are in some sense their own.

In addition to taking a closer look at the parables of Jesus and the significance that Jesus himself placed on story, in recent years, many scholars have taken an interest in narrative as a way of interpreting Scripture. While scholars have long noted the different types of literature found in the Bible – poems, songs, letters, wisdom literature, etc. – paying attention to narrative means that the reader will focus on such things as plot and characters and the reader is encouraged to experience something of the sacred through an interaction with the text.[12] The Bible is not read as dogma or history, attention is given to the story and the reader's engagement with it.

One important aspect of using a literary approach to Scripture is that attention is given to the subtle differences in the way stories are told and how they are placed in the Gospels. This means, for instance, that in reading the Gospels, we must take seriously the fact that the Gospel writers were repeating the stories of Jesus to specific groups of people and using them to address particular situations. For example, readers of Mark's Gospel will know that it has been suggested that it was not written in Palestine because often the author feels the need to explain Jewish traditions to an unfamiliar audience.[13] On the other hand, Matthew's Gospel appears to have been written to Jewish Christians and the writer is at great pains to insist that Jewish heritage should not be abandoned. Hence, in Matthew's Gospel, Jesus says that he came to fulfil the law, not abolish it (Matthew 5.17); words that are not found in Mark's account.

All of the Gospel writers gave attention to the plot. Luke for example suggests that Jesus was on a journey, which is to be understood not so much a geographical one as a journey to the cross, while Mark makes the passion of Christ the focus of the whole Gospel. Yet, it was John who used symbol and story to weave together a Gospel which was quite different from the other three. Some of the stories told in the other Gospel accounts are not included in John. For example, there is no mention of casting out demons or healing lepers in John's Gospel. In fact, the miracle stories are named as 'signs' which indicate that Jesus was to be seen as the Son of God. The differences between the Gospels are interesting to note and clearly a cursory reading of them points to the fact that we have a different arrangement of the stories of Jesus in each Gospel. In fact, the fourth Evangelist openly makes the point that there are 'many other things that Jesus did; if every one of them were written down, I suppose the world itself could not contain the books that would be written' (John

21.25). In part, what this affirms is that the Gospel writers have taken some of the stories of Jesus and put them together in a pattern that would speak to the communities to which they were writing.

All of this highlights an important point when thinking about the Bible as story and its place in Christian spirituality. Reading Scripture is not simply an exercise in learning and discovering facts about Jesus or finding texts we believe will support particular doctrinal viewpoints or cultural ideals. Rather Scripture is story to be entered into and we are to interact with the text. Christians believe that the Word is living and the Gospel stories call people to an encounter or to an interaction between the Bible story and our stories, as individuals and as communities of faith. Christian tradition argues that it is always the Spirit who gives life and speaks words of life to people.

While some people may feel uneasy with an approach to Scripture that looks closely at issues such as plot and authorial intent, one could argue that recognition of the power of narrative is simply to follow in the steps of Jesus. Indeed, used alongside other approaches to interpreting the biblical text, and with a willingness to listen in a way in which we ourselves are vulnerable, accepting, expectant, and constant, the narrative approach can provide great insight into the Bible.[14] Storytelling, of course, is not simply a matter of relating an event – it is about seeking after truth that is beyond the story itself.

Storytelling in the Church

Perhaps because of a fear that the authority of the Bible may be diminished by any approach to Scripture other than what is considered to be a literal reading of the text, some people may shy away from this narrative approach. Yet, clearly, even Jesus did not use language in a way that was always to be taken literally, for example when he said to his disciples, 'It is easier for a camel to go through the eye of a needle than for someone who is rich to enter the kingdom of God' (Mark 10.25). The stories he told were offered as a way of drawing people closer to God. The use of narrative, which was very much a part of the culture of his day, was a way of conveying truth that was beyond language. While often people wanted to live by the letter of the law, no doubt Jesus' desire was for people to listen and feel where the words came from.

Not only was story central to Jesus' approach to teaching and critical to the formation of early Christian communities, but hearing the stories of believers down through the ages has been central to the creation of the Church. From the beginning, the stories of Christians have been told as a way of encouraging others in the way of Christ. In the Letter to the Hebrews, the reader is admonished to walk 'by faith' in the way of Abraham, Isaac, Jacob, Moses, etc. In remembering that they are surrounded by 'so great a cloud of witnesses' Christians are to 'run the race' set before them (Hebrews 11.4—12.4). Likewise in the early Church stories were told of those who gladly faced martyrdom for their beliefs. No doubt the story of Polycarp, the old bishop of Smyrna in AD 155 was told time and time again as a way of setting an example for those who followed.

> Now, as he was entering the stadium, there came to Polycarp a voice from heaven, 'Be strong, Polycarp, and play the man' . . . Thereupon he was led forth, and great was the uproar of them that heard that Polycarp had been seized . . . But the Proconsul urged him and said, 'Swear, and I will release thee; curse the Christ.' And Polycarp said, 'Eighty and six years have I served him, and he hath done me no wrong; how then can I blaspheme my king who saved me?' . . . They were about to nail him to the stake, when he said, 'Let me be as I am. He that granted me to endure the fire will grant me also to remain at the pyre unmoved, without being secured with nails.' When he had ended his prayer the firemen lighted the fire. And a great flame flashed forth: and we, to whom it was given to see, beheld a marvel . . . the fire took the shape of a vault, like a ship's sail bellying in the wind, and it made a wall round the martyr's body and there was the body; in the midst, like a loaf being baked or like gold and silver being tried in the furnace . . .[15]

As this story and others like it were told and retold among the Christians, they served as a reminder of the faith of those who had gone before them. The truth of the story was not so much in the detail as in the faith it sought to convey. When exploring Christian spirituality, great care must be taken when examining spiritual texts. Alister McGrath helpfully points out that the objective of reading a classic is to read it not as a 'passive spectator', but as an 'active participant'.[16] He then includes a helpful checklist of questions which might be asked as one begins to engage with a text: 'Who is the author? For whom was the text written? What is the historical and cultural context of the work? What biblical imagery does the work employ? What does the writer want me to think? What does the writer want me to do? What can I take away from engagement with the text?'[17] McGrath acknowledges that these questions are just a starting point for engagement with the text, but they provide an initial plan or framework for exploration.

While exploring texts, it is also useful to keep in mind the many and varied ways that stories function. In his book, *Storytelling: Imagination and Faith*, W. J. Bausch has highlighted the way stories provide a bridge to our roots and to our common humanity. In addition, he claims that story gives people a language by which they may articulate dreams and hopes and longings that they may not otherwise be able to put into words. Drawing from the work of Robert Bela Wilhelm, Bausch says we use at least three kinds of talk in our common experience: 1) daytime talk, 2) night-time talk, 3) storytelling.[18] Daytime talk, according to Bausch, is the language of declarative sentences. We may speak to one another about the weather, or describe a football match, or relate the events of a day at work. Night-time talk, however, is a way of describing the language of hopes and aspirations. It is the kind that we find difficult to put into words because it expresses some of our deepest fears and longings. For example, we may have hoped for years that we would have reconciliation with another person. Or perhaps we desperately want life to be different. We may find these kinds of feelings hard to explain and certainly not something that we would find we could easily speak of to another. Story-telling, according to Bausch, bridges these two types of talk. It provides a way to give voice to things we would otherwise find hard to express. In this way, story leads us closer to others and perhaps more deeply into ourselves.[19] Claiming with Bishop John Robinson that the approach to truth 'starts from life rather than dogma' he concludes that 'life is made up of wild dreams, half-seen visions, impulses and nameless shadows which we relate in our stories'.[20]

In addition to noting that story provides us with a way of communicating some of our deepest longings, Stanley Hauerwas has pointed out that narrative accounts bind 'events and agents together' in an understandable pattern.[21] A Christian's relationship to God is portrayed in narrative: the story of Jesus of Nazareth. In the Christian tradition, the 'Christ story' as opposed to doctrines is said to become the dominant organizing pattern in the life of the believer and the community. The idea that Christ is the dominating story is central to how narrative might be used in Christian spirituality today. As Christians study the Bible, they are not to approach it as if they are simply searching for dogmatic truth, rather they are to come to it with an openness to discovering what it means to be transfigured and transformed in the likeness of Christ. Perhaps it might be said that their story is to be shaped by the story of the Christ.

Storytelling within a community enables us to share and interpret our experience of life and relationship. It is a basic premise of this book that storytelling is an integral part of Christian spirituality. Hence, the Christian tradition teaches that we learn about God through the stories found in the Bible, in the celebration of Eucharist (as a rehearsal of the story of salvation), as well as in our relationship with God, others and the wider realm of nature. As we share our stories and hear the stories of others we may reflect on Christian spirituality.

Draw your own conclusions

Identify stories (positive and negative) which have shaped the way you understand your nation, local community, or family. How have these stories shaped identity?

Reflect on Steere's characteristics of a good listener: vulnerability, acceptance, expectancy and constancy. How might these characteristics of listening be applied to a spiritual text or to Scripture?

Explore the power of narrative to shape and transform. How might story shape the uncompleted?

Further reading

Narrative and the art of storytelling

Wendell Berry (2000), *Jayber Crow*, New York: Counterpoint.

Wendell Berry (2004), *That Distant Land: The Collected Stories of Wendell Berry*, Emeryville, California: Shoemaker & Hoard.

Wendell Berry (2005), 'The Burden of the Gospels', in *The Way of Ignorance and Other Essays*, Emeryville, California: Shoemaker & Hoard.

Frederick Buechner (1977), *Telling the Truth: The Gospel as Tragedy, Comedy and Fairy Tale*, New York: Harper & Row.

Frederick Buechner (1981), *The Alphabet of Grace*, New York: The Seabury Press.

Jerome Bruner (1986), *Actual Minds, Possible Worlds*, Cambridge, MA: Harvard University Press.

Jerome Bruner (2002), *Making Stories*, New York: Farrar, Strauss & Giroux.

Annie Dillard (1974), *Pilgrim at Tinker Creek*, New York: Harper's Magazine Press.

Annie Dillard (1977), *Holy the Firm*, New York: Harper & Row.

Annie Dillard (1987), *An American Childhood*, New York: Harper & Row.

John S. Dunne (1967/69), *A Search for God in Time and Memory*, London: Sheldon Press.

John S. Dunne (1973), *Time and Myth: A Meditation on Storytelling as an Exploration of Life and Death*, London: SCM Press.

John S. Dunne (1982/1983), *The Church of the Poor Devil: Reflections On*

A Riverboat Voyage and A Spiritual Journal, Notre Dame, Indiana: Notre Dame University Press.

John S. Dunne (1987), *The Homing Spirit*, New York: Crossroad.

T. M. Leitch (1986), *What Stories Are: Narrative Theory and Interpretation*, University Park: Pennsylvania State University Press.

James Wm. McClendon Jr. (1974/1990), *Biography as Theology: How Life Stories Can Remake Today's Theology*, Philadelphia: Trinity Press International.

Margaret Reid MacDonald (1993), *The Story-teller's Start-Up Book*, Little Rock, Arkansas: August House Publishers.

Eugene H. Peterson (1994/1997), *Subversive Spirituality*, Grand Rapids: William Eerdmans.

Annette Simmons (2002), *The Story Factor: Inspiration, Influence and Persuasion through the Art of Storytelling*, New York: Basic Books.

Approaching a spiritual text

E. Glenn Hinson (1968), *Seekers After Mature Faith*, Waco, Texas: Word.

Alister E. McGrath (1999), *Christian Spirituality, An Introduction*, Oxford: Blackwell, pp. 138–9.

Philip Sheldrake (1991), *Spirituality and History*, London: SPCK, pp. 163–87.

Notes

1 *Becoming A Jew – Who Do You Think You Are? Family Ties*, BBC 4, 12 October 2004, directed and filmed by Emily Conroy.

2 John Seely Brown, Stephen Denning, Katalina Groh and Laurence Prusak (2005), *Storytelling in Organizations: Why Storytelling is Transforming 21st Century Organizations and Management*, Oxford: Elsevier Butterworth-Heinemann.

3 The universality of narrative may be seen across cultural and religious divides.

4 Two examples of this kind of link to the past are the annual St Patrick's Day celebration in Boston by those of Irish descent and the 'Burns night suppers' held in many places around the world each January by those who are of Scottish ancestry.

5 Margaret Forster (1986), *Significant Sisters: The Grass Roots of Active Feminism, 1839–1939*, Harmondsworth: Penguin Books.

6 An Oratorio, *The Song of Terezín* written by Franz Waxman, is based on poems written by children interned at the Terezín ghetto. *I Never Saw Another Butterfly*, a play written by Celeste Raspanti, is the story of one of the 15,000 children who passed through Terezín. The play is based on collected poems and drawings by those children, which were recovered and published in a book of the same name by Hana Volavkova.

7 This idea is discussed in an article by Stephen Crites (1971), 'The Narrative Quality of Experience', *Journal of the American Academy of Religion*, Vol. 39, No. 3, September, pp. 291–311.

8 Douglas V. Steere (1955), *On Listening to Another*, San Francisco: Harper & Row, p. vii.

9 Steere, *Listening*, p. 12.

10 Steere, *Listening*, p. 14.

11 The discussion of the approaches to the interpretation of Scripture is beyond the bounds of this chapter. However, many scholarly works have been written on approaches to the interpretation of Scripture. See, for instance, Kevin J. Vanhoozer (1998), *Is There a Meaning in this Text? The Bible, The Reader, and the Morality of Literary Knowledge*, Leicester: Apollos/Inter-Varsity Press, and John Goldingay (1995), *Models for the Interpretation of Scripture*, Grand Rapids, Michigan: William Eerdmans.

12 The narrative approach is discussed in George W. Stroup (1981), *The Promise of Narrative Theology*, London: SCM Press, and Roger Standing (2004), *Finding the Plot, Preaching in Narrative Style*, Milton Keynes: Paternoster Press. For a readable introduction to a narrative approach to the Gospel of Luke, see Fred B. Craddock (1990), *Luke, Interpretation, A Bible Commentary for Preaching and Teaching*, Louisville: John Knox Press, pp. 1–10.

13 Scholars do not agree on the place of authorship. See the discussion in Francis J. Maloney (2004), *Mark, Storyteller, Interpreter, Evangelist*, Peabody, Mass: Hendrickson Publishers, pp. 9–14, and for a readable introduction to narrative criticism applied to the Gospel, pp. 31–8.

14 A whole style of narrative preaching has developed using this approach. See Standing, *Finding the Plot*; Eugene L. Lowry (1980), *The Homiletical Plot, The Sermon as Narrative Art Form*, Atlanta: John Knox Press; Thomas G. Long (1989), *Preaching and the Literary Forms of the Bible*, Philadelphia: Fortress Press; and Thomas E. Boomershine (1988), *Story Journey: An Invitation to the Gospel as Storytelling*, Nashville: Abingdon Press.

15 'The Martyrdom of Polycarp', in Henry Bettenson (1973), *Documents of the Christian Church*, 2nd edn, London: Oxford University Press, pp. 10–11.

16 Alister E. McGrath (1999), *Christian Spirituality: An Introduction*, Oxford: Blackwell, p. 138.

17 McGrath, *Christian Spirituality*, pp. 138–40.

18 William J. Bausch (1984), *Storytelling: Imagination and Faith*, Mystic, Connecticut: Twenty-third Publications, p. 38.

19 Bausch, *Storytelling*, p. 38.

20 Bausch, *Storytelling*, p. 19.

21 Stanley Hauerwas (1977), *Truthfulness and Tragedy*, Notre Dame, Indiana: University of Notre Dame Press, p. 8 as cited in Stroup, *Promise*, p. 79. For other work by Hauerwas on the use of narrative, see John Berkman and Michael Cartwright (eds) (2001), *The Hauerwas Reader*, Durham, N.C. and London: Duke University Press, especially pp. 165–266, and Stanley Hauerwas and L. Gregory Jones (eds) (1989), *Why Narrative?: Readings in Narrative Theology*, Grand Rapids: William Eerdmans.

3

Patterns of Christian Community

I know a lovely woman, Eliza, who lives in Kosova. When fighting disturbed the peace of that place, she and her family fled to Macedonia. She had no job, no way of providing for her family. After many weeks of struggling to find food for her family, one night she prayed: 'O God you have abandoned me and my family.' In response to her prayer, Eliza said that she heard a voice saying, 'I have not abandoned you; tomorrow is a new day.' The next day, after searching all day for food, she prayed again: 'O God you have abandoned me and my family' and again she said that she heard the reply: 'I have not abandoned you; tomorrow is a new day.' The next day, as she searched for food for her family, she met a woman who told her she knew of Christians in the area who might help her. That day the Christians came to see Eliza and her family and gave them food and financial assistance. Yet, Eliza says that most importantly, she found a new community. When she visited the Christian church, and met the Christians who had gathered there for worship, she felt as if she had always known them. She had discovered a place of belonging.

Eliza's discovery of relationship and community is not unique to Christian faith. The need for a place to be and to become as well as the need to belong is part of the human experience. All living things exist in relationship: plants, animals, human beings exist in a balance of belonging. The types of relationship we have differ; our relationship to pets is not the same as our relationship to friends and family. Yet, the need to exist 'in relation to' something is central to any living thing.

One way to speak of living relationally is to speak of being in community. Communities, of course, are not all based on close relationships. The term 'community' is sometimes used to refer to a geographical location such as a village or town. For instance, one may speak of a village community, a neighbourhood community or a fishing community. Community may be used also to refer to some 'relational' connection which draws people to one another. This might be a group of people with a common background, history, and heritage or shared interest. Living in close proximity, or sharing common tasks, however, does not necessarily mean that people are building deep bonds of kinship. Yet in community, as David McMillan has suggested, there is some sense of belonging:

sense of community is a feeling that members have of belonging, a feeling that members matter to one another and to the group, and a shared faith that members' needs will be met through their commitment to be together.[1]

There are, of course, many factors which influence our feeling of 'belonging' within a community and not all communities provide a positive sense of association. Some groups are created to exclude or to wield power or influence in negative ways. Other communities are based on rather superficial or casual social contacts which deny the richer sense of relatedness that real belonging implies. Wendell Berry, an American author, has explored the depth of genuine relatedness amongst the characters that live in a fictional community which he calls Port William. At first it may seem that community in Port William is mainly territorial because the characters all live in the same geographical area and share a love for the land. Yet, a closer reading explores a much deeper sense of belonging to one another. The membership of Port William includes the living and the dead. They are part of one another; members of one another. They have shared in work and life. In the novel *Hannah Coulter*, an elderly lady looks back on her life and reflects on the belonging in the membership that she has known with family, friends and place.

> The membership had an economic purpose and it had an economic result, but the purpose and the result were more than economic ... There was no bookkeeping, no accounting, no settling up. What you owed was considered paid when you had done what needed doing. Every account was paid in full by the understanding that when we were needed we would go, and when we had need the others, or enough of them would come ... The members, I guess you could say, are born into it, they stay in it by choosing to stay, and they die in it. Or they leave it, as my children have done.[2]

The fact that her children left 'the membership' worried Hannah. It was not that she did not understand their desire to 'move up'. Since she did not have a chance at formal education, she wanted her children to have it. But later, after they left Port William she worried that somehow in her own telling of the stories to her children when they were small, she had not fully conveyed the deep wonder at belonging to a place and to others.

But did we tell the stories right? It was lovely, the telling and the listening, usually the last thing before bedtime. But did we tell the stories in such a way as to suggest that we had needed a better chance or a better life or a better place than we had? I don't know, but I have had to ask. Suppose your stories, instead of mourning and rejoicing over the past, say that everything should have been different. Suppose you encourage or even just allow your children to believe that their parents ought to have been different people, with a better chance, born in a better place. Or suppose the stories you tell them allow them to believe, when they hear it from other people, that farming people are inferior and need to improve themselves by leaving the farm. Doesn't that finally unmake everything that has been made? Isn't that the loose thread that unravels the whole garment? And how are you ever to know where the thread breaks, and when the tug begins?[3]

Hannah's reflections on belonging are central to Christian spirituality. The longing to be in relationship to God, others and the wider universe is at the heart of Christian faith. While the starting point for Christian belief is sometimes described in terms of an individual response to God, it is a central tenet of the Christian faith that a person is never a believer in isolation, but is always part of a wider community of faith.

The importance of relationship to Christian spirituality has at times been undermined by a focus on doctrinal correctness or on individual experience. Among some Christian groups, a concern for signs of a true experience and a stress upon individual 'conversion' has sometimes over-shadowed the important understanding of knowing God in community. When community is emphasized, it is often defined in doctrinal or even institutional language which does not always allow for the kind of diversity and difference which is part of participation in the life of God. To say: 'he is a Calvinist' or 'she is Catholic' or 'they are evangelicals' or 'they are Pentecostals or Anglicans' suggests that there is only one inter-pretation of those labels. Moreover, it stresses only one aspect of an ap-proach to spirituality and does not reflect deeper issues of unity in Christ. The tendency to divide people by denominations or label them according to theological views does not reflect the biblical understanding of com-munity in Christ. In the words of Apostle Paul: 'There is no longer Jew or Greek, there is no longer slave or free, there is no longer male and female;' (and we might add there is no longer liberal or evangelical; Catholic or Baptist; Methodist or Quaker!) 'for all of you are one in Christ Jesus' (Galatians 3.28).

There are different relational descriptions of Christian community in Scripture, such as 'the body the Christ', a 'pilgrim people', a 'people of God'. These images, as Stanley Hauerwas points out, 'denote the social reality of being Christian and what it means to be a distinctive people formed by the narrative of God'.[4] Church, as community sharing in the life of God, is not simply about being together in order to alleviate loneliness or answer a longing for friendship. Rather the Church as community is in relationship because of Christ. Real community, therefore, is based on presence, not the presence of one person to another, but the presence of Christ within the world. So, if Christ is present then true community in Christ is not dependent on any outward institutional form or cherished belief. The understanding that bonds of relationship may extend beyond any difference of human understanding led the Roman Catholic, Thomas Merton, for example, to live a solitary life as a Cistercian monk, and at the same time to engage deeply with the world. It led him to reach beyond the bounds of his tradition to establish friendships with Southern Baptists and Buddhist monks. He believed that real unity in Christ went beyond doctrinal formulae. He wrote:

> This obsession with doctrinal formulas, juridical order and ritual exactitude has often made people forget that the heart of Catholicism, too, is a living experience of unity in Christ which far transcends all conceptual formulations.[5]

Merton did not begin the Christian life with this belief. He embraced the Roman Catholic faith in 1938 and in 1941 he entered the Abbey of Gethsemani, in Kentucky, a community of monks belonging to the Order of Cistercians of the Strict Observance (Trappists), which is one of the most ascetic Roman Catholic monastic orders. At this point, it would seem that he was withdrawing from the world in order to give himself to God, something he saw in rather narrowly defined terms. Later, he came to the realization that because of Christ, bonds of relationship were possible with people who did not share with him a common life or belief. Surprisingly, he made this discovery one day while standing on a street corner in Louisville, Kentucky. Merton described his experience in this way:

> In Louisville, at the corner of Fourth and Walnut, in the center of the shopping district, I was suddenly overwhelmed with the realization that I loved all of those people, that they were mine and I theirs . . . It was like waking from a dream of separateness . . . this sense of liberation . . . could have taken form in the words: 'Thank God, thank God that I am like other men, that I am only a man among others.'[6]

Mark Gibbard once commented that this experience was Merton's 'second conversion'. Merton, claimed Gibbard, had first been converted to 'God transcendent, God the Lord of all. In the shopping district of Louisville he was converted to the world or rather to God immanent in his world and in his people.'[7] What Merton discovered is that the deep bonds of relationship which the New Testament refers to as 'union in Christ' have little to do with physical proximity or long conversation. Some of the deepest connections are wordless. They are not dependent on attendance at worship services, though worship with others is an important part of spirituality and may increase our awareness of the multi-faceted nature of Christ. Yet true community in Christ, because it 'transfigures absence', is not disturbed by the physical absence of another.[8]

Christ's presence may be discovered in the ordinary things of life as well as the extraordinary. This sense of living in and through and with Christ at all times and in all places is expressed in the prayer of St Patrick (AD 389–461):

> Christ, be with me, Christ before me, Christ behind me,
> Christ in me, Christ beneath me, Christ above me,
> Christ on my right, Christ on my left,
> Christ where I lie, Christ where I sit,
> Christ where I arise,
> Christ in the heart of every one who thinks of me,
> Christ in the mouth of every one who speaks to me,
> Christ in every eye that sees me,
> Christ in every ear that hears me . . .[9]

It is Christ who is head of the body, the Church. Christ who shares in their meals. Christ who is present in every situation and circumstance of their lives. Community is based on the presence of Christ.

In order to describe this idea of knowing Christ in and through all things, the Apostle Paul used repeated references to being 'in Christ'. M. A. Seifrid points out that when it is used in the New Testament Epistles, the phrase 'in Christ' is used with little distinction between 'locality, instrumentality and modality'.[10] Sometimes the Apostle Paul seems to be referring to certain churches in a particular locality that are in Christ. At other times Christ is seen as an instrument of action: 'in Christ, God was reconciling the world to himself' (2 Corinthians 5.19). Sometimes the expression is used to denote a mode of speech: 'I am speaking the truth in Christ' (Romans 9.1). While there has been some scholarly debate about the meaning of being 'in Christ', generally speaking, when used by Christians it is commonly understood as meaning that they have a deep relatedness to others because they share in union with Christ, through his death and resurrection. This emphasis on relationship with Christ who is present leads us to explore the biblical understanding of God who is in and through all things and beyond them, too. For the significance of relationship to God in community takes us to the very heart of the nature of God.

God as Trinity: the heart of community

In recent years scholars have explored the fundamental notion that to be made in the image of God is to be made in the image of community who is God. Miroslav Volf explores the way an understanding of God as Trinity might inform our understanding of relationships among people within the Christian Church and in relation to wider community as well. Admittedly there are many different ways in which the Church has expressed itself as an institution. Different interpretations of leadership and authority within the Church have led to very different patterns of ecclesiology. Volf looks specifically at his understanding of the Church as a 'gathered community' and suggests that the vision of the Church is nothing less than 'the image of a triune God'.[11] By way of dialogue with Roman Catholic and Orthodox ecclesiology, Volf suggests that 'the presence of Christ, which constitutes the church' is mediated through the whole congregation and not simply through ordained ministers.[12] In short, he suggests that the Church should be a reflection of the very nature of God as Trinity; a people in communion with God who reflect the very nature of the One who is love in relationship.

Likewise, other scholars have explored the notion of God as Trinity and the way this may inform our understanding of the Church. Colin Gunton, for instance, examined the way an 'immanent trinity' might be reflected in the Church.[13] He suggested that the Church should 'echo the dynamic relations between the three persons who constitute the deity'.[14] The Church, he claimed, 'is called to be the kind of reality at a finite level that God is in eternity . . . the eternal becoming of God – the eternally inter-animating energies of the three – to provide the basis for the personal dynamics of the community'.[15] Paul Fiddes likens the relationship of the Trinity to a dance and suggests that 'the image of the dance makes most sense when we understand the divine persons as movements of relationship, rather than as individual subjects who have relationships'.[16] 'So, the image of the divine dance is not so much about dancers as about the patterns of the dance itself, an interweaving of ecstatic movements.'[17]

Great care must be taken, of course, if it sounds like all this talk of reflecting God as Trinity means perfect unity within the Church. The pages of church history do not need to be turned too far to find examples of disharmony, especially over the way one describes God as Trinity![18] Indeed, Christian community, if it reflects the nature of a Triune God, is not simply about unity, but also includes difference and diversity. David Cunningham explains this diversity in terms of 'particularity'.[19] He suggests that he does not mean particular in the terms of singular or individual, rather, he uses the term to talk about the relational nature of the Trinity.[20] David Cunningham warns against applying a simple understanding of relationality to our understanding of the Trinity. In other words, when we speak of relationship, as he points out, people speak of separate identities and relationship between two separate entities. This, of course, is not what Christians understand by God who is Trinity. Rather as Cunningham points out, God is 'wholly constituted by relationality'. 'God is relation without remainder.' Hence, he describes 'the Trinitarian virtue of participation' as the key to understanding what it might mean for us to 'dwell in and be indwelt by' others in genuine relationship.[21]

The implications of embracing the idea of God as Trinity-in-community or rather 'participating in God' are far-reaching for Christian theology and challenge the Christian Church's views on issues such as authority, leadership, and ecumenism and a lot more besides.[22] The purpose of our discussion here, however, is not to enter into a theological discussion about the Trinity, but to note that the image of 'God in community' serves as a reminder that Christian experience is never to be understood only as a personal journey. Christians are always believers together – a community bound together in the love of God. Indeed, of fundamental importance to Christian spirituality is a life in community sharing 'life together in Christ'.

Life together in community

Even a cursory reading of the Acts of the Apostles indicates that for the early Christians, life in relation to other believers was central. The followers of Jesus 'devoted themselves to the apostles' teaching and fellowship, to the breaking of bread and the prayers' (Acts 2.42). The fellowship which they enjoyed was clearly much more than simply shared interests or experience. These gatherings for fellowship or in the assembly (Greek: *ekklesia*) known as the Church clearly were not simply gatherings for public prayer or the reading of the word. Rather in their relationship to one another 'in Christ' they discovered a deep sense of belonging.

The New Testament uses many different images for the Church, but by and large they are all relational images. Moreover, there is a central focus on a tangible union, a oneness in the love of Christ. The many parts of the body are bound together in love, which never fails (1 Corinthians 12.1—13.13). Naturally, the outward expression of the Church or forms of ecclesiology have been debated and discussed throughout the years. In the early Christian Church there was great difference with regard to 'custom and attitude and in theological expression'.[23] While at times there have been attempts to portray the Church in idealized terms 'as if it were characterized by complete unanimity and possessing a single mind on all subjects', this was far from the case.[24]

By the fourth century, when Constantine embraced Christian faith, the Church joined hands with the state and from this point on, the Church became inextricably linked to culture. This would mean that the way the Church saw itself as community would change as well. While the Church no longer experienced persecution by the state, it continued to face doctrinal disputes over issues of authority relating to leadership, and the person and nature of Christ. Between 325 and 787 there were seven ecumenical councils of the Church which sought to establish foundational teaching on what were considered to be fundamental doctrines. Before long, different patterns of church life began to form in the East and in the West and in 1054 a clear division between East and West became apparent in the Church. There had long been signs of disquiet between the two, but the difference of opinion was brought to a head by the unwillingness of the Bishop of Rome to recognize the authority of ecumenical councils of the Church and a doctrinal dispute over the way one speaks of God as Holy Spirit. Yet, the division represented more than simply two different understandings of ecclesiology or the relationship between ecclesial and political powers. There were differences in theology and worship which reflected diverse social and political cultures.

By the sixteenth century the Church in the West was increasingly challenged by a number of different calls for reform from both inside and outside the Church. One of the continuing issues to emerge in this period was the call to discover the nature of the true Church. For some, 'Protestants' as they came to be known, the Church was to be defined by the right proclamation of word and sacrament. Many within the Roman Catholic Church felt that tradition – particularly as it related to issues of leadership and authority – must not be ignored. It is, of course, important to remember that the discussion and division within the Church cannot be put down merely to disparity in theological views. Anytime the Church has faced conflict, the cause has never been simply arising from intellectual variances of opinion, but included social, economic and political causes for dissension. Yet the differences over their understanding of the authority of the Church – among other things to dictate doctrine and to interpret Scripture – were evident and eventually resulted in division.

Since these divisions of the Western Christian Church, it has divided again and again with each different group claiming to reflect the true body of Christ. While often these expressions of Christian faith have begun out of disenchantment with an institutional structure, eventually the move from 'prophecy to order'[25] results in the Church being identified with what H. Richard Niebuhr called 'the Christ of culture'.[26] The move toward institutionalizing faith is in some ways a clear sign of the desire to explain (or cynically perhaps to control) faith.

By the early twentieth century there were many different Christian groups and denominations. Some of these, although very diverse, had been co-operating on projects for mission and evangelism for some time. In 1910, they decided to hold a World Missionary Conference in Edinburgh in order to discuss matters of faith and unity which had previously kept them apart. At this meeting, over 1,200 delegates representing many Christian groups met together to discuss greater co-operation between missionary societies. This meeting was followed by further conferences in Lausanne and Edinburgh in 1927 and 1937, respectively, where various doctrinal issues relating to 'life and work' and 'faith and order' were discussed. The meetings were not attended by representatives of the Russian Orthodox Church or the Roman Catholic Church, but nevertheless represented a real attempt to move toward greater co-operation among many Christians. By 1948 the World Council of Churches was formed at a meeting held at Amsterdam. The stated constitutional purpose of the World Council of Churches is to be 'a fellowship of churches which confess the Lord Jesus Christ as God and Saviour according to the Scriptures and therefore seek to fulfill together their common calling to the glory of the one God, Father, Son and Holy Spirit.'[27] Today the council includes churches from different cultural backgrounds and Christian traditions, including Orthodox churches and Christians from nearly every Protestant tradition.[28] One of the greatest challenges to the World Council of Churches, as Michael Kinnamon has described it, is finding the 'limits of both unity and diversity'.[29] Kinnamon points out that it is possible to have a 'unity' which does not reflect community. This is the type of unity which is held together by domination and control.

Real community, however, as he points out, is based on people being freely and fully present to one another.[30]

Although the World Council of Churches does not represent a formal unity between Roman Catholics and other Christians, since the early 1960s, there have been strides toward engagement and dialogue between various groups. In 1958 when Pope John XXIII came to the papal office, he took steps toward Christians outside the Roman Catholic Church. He called together a council of the Church and invited Protestant observers to attend. Thus Vatican II, as the council came to be called, which met from 1962 to 1965, marked the beginning of a new ecumenicity and also addressed issues such as liturgical renewal and the importance of dialogue between the Church and the modern world. Steps were taken toward greater unity as well. The council of Vatican II began to explore the nature of the Church and affirmed what they described as the 'mystery of the Church' and while stressing the hierarchical government of the Church, it likewise spoke of the Church as the 'people of God' and a 'pilgrim people'.[31]

After Vatican II, Catholic theologians continued to reflect on the nature of the Christian Church. Hans Küng wrote *The Church Maintained in Truth* in which he claimed that Christians are 'confident that there is a living God and that in the future this God will also maintain their believing community in life and truth'.[32] The openness which Küng displayed was not appreciated by all Roman Catholics and some did not welcome the changes in liturgy or the steps toward co-operation with other Christians. Yet, since Vatican II, the Roman Catholic Church has continued, in varying degrees, the discussion about the nature of the Church and looked to cultivate relationships with other Christians.

A vision for unity: Brother Roger and Taizé

The move toward greater co-operation in the Church – with ecumenical discussion both within and outside the Catholic Church – has meant that some Christians have promoted a vision of unity which would enable Christians to live together in a way that would transcend denominational distinctions. This vision of unity has found many different expressions across the years, but one embodiment of it is the Taizé community which was founded in 1940 in Burgundy in France by Roger Schutz-Marsauche. The Taizé community began because Brother Roger, as he came to be known, had a passion for unity and could not understand why animosity should exist between Christians. His desire was to create a community where 'kindness of heart would be a matter of practical experience, and where love would be at the heart of all things'.[33] Describing the beginnings of the community, Brother Roger later wrote of:

> a small vulnerable community, held up by an irrational hope, the hope of creating harmony between the children of baptism and children everywhere; a community of seventy men, Christians called on to do a task which is quite beyond them, and who in spite of limited numbers, try to answer every appeal made to them, no matter from what direction.[34]

Brother Roger's vision, indeed, his whole approach to community in Christ, was shaped by the belief that God is not limited by doctrine or denomination and that people are made for communion with God and one another. He said that Christ is known in the mystery of communion which is the Church. Yet, this communion does not come without struggle and contemplation.

Brother Roger was killed in 2005 in a public meeting. 'Today, the Taizé Community is made up of over a hundred brothers, Catholics and from various Protestant backgrounds, coming from more than twenty-five nations. By its very existence, the community is thus a concrete sign of reconciliation between divided Christians and separated peoples.'[35]

In the twenty-first century, Christians have continued to struggle to understand how the Church is to be a community of faith. In an age when the Internet has introduced the notion of instant communication through chat-rooms and 'blog' sites, the Christian Church is challenged to think again about what it means to be a people who are a community of faith. Some Christians have argued that old forms of worship and ways of gathering and relating to one another must be replaced by different forms of communication which include video links and virtual worship services. The danger with such approaches is that they minimize the importance of a place of belonging and the need for a community of presence. There are Christians today who believe that if they can sustain a lively pattern of worship or plan activities that will bring people together they will have discovered what it means to be the Church. Yet, the key question for those seeking to understand Christian community is not what form should worship take, but rather, what does it mean to live in relationship to God and one another?

The answer to this question, as we have already noted, has resulted in the formation of many different Christian groups and expressions of ecclesiology. There are many different historical examples of community life: from the stories of early groups of believers in the New Testament, to stories of other kinds of communities which formed out of a desire to give themselves more truly to the way of Christ. Each of these has something to teach us about the nature of Christian community. Many believed that they were forming themselves according to the New Testament pattern; most of them were searching for the true Church. All of them, perhaps, realized that at the heart of their longing for God was the desire for relationship.

Sometimes the search for the true Church has led to exclusion rather than inclusion in Christian community. Among early Christians there were a number of doctrinal debates which led to Christians excluding others. In North Africa in the fourth century, for example, Augustine had to face division among rival Christian communities. Each community, as Henry Chadwick points out, 'made the exclusive claim to be the one mystical body of Christ and the sole ark of salvation, the Mother without whom one cannot have God as one's Father'.[36] One community, the Donatists, rejected the validity of the sacraments other than their own, which in effect meant that they did not recognize others outside their group as Christian in any sense.

This tendency toward exclusiveness on doctrinal grounds can be seen throughout history. To cite another example, the Puritans in the seventeenth century, and many who have drawn from their Calvinist view of covenant theology have, unfortunately, employed language which has implied that they were more interested in creating a 'fence' to keep people in, than forming an 'open gate' by which people were free to come and go.

Over the years, as various other Christian groups formed and re-formed, some have placed more emphasis on uniformity of doctrine or belief while others have tended to stress the necessity of shared experience. On the other hand, there have also been groups which have rejected any prescribed doctrinal formula, ritual or convention as the basis for life together. The Shakers, for instance, or as they were more formally called, the United Society of Believers in Christ's Second Appearing, who were founded by Mother Anne Lee in the eighteenth century in England, shunned formal institutional religion and built communities based on simplicity and equality. They established communities in America in the nineteenth century and became known for their simple songs, their rhythmical dances in worship and their creativity and they were responsible, among other things, for flat brooms, wooden clothes pins and washing machines. While many Christians would disagree with some of their theological views, their vision of simplicity touches at the heart of

Christian faith. For them, simplicity was a gift from God and central to the Christian way. They sang about it in this way:

'Tis the Gift to be simple
'Tis the gift to be free
'Tis the gift to come down where we ought to be
And when we find ourselves in the place just right,
'Twill be in the valley of love and delight.
When true simplicity is gained
To bow and to bend we shan't be ashamed
To turn, turn will be our delight
Till by turning and turning we come round right.[37]

The Shakers believed that the call to simplicity could be heard in the Gospel stories which appealed to people to make God and God alone the desire of their hearts. Likewise, for them, true simplicity was only fully realized in authentic Christian community where the whole of life, even labour, was worship and prayer. At the heart of their approach to spirituality was the belief that living in Christ and living in community were one. Hence simplicity was not something which was received as one gave up material goods or the longing for personal gain. Rather it was discovered as one gave oneself to others in and through life together in the body of Christ. 'The interests of one are to be the interests of all' they declared as they sought to build communities based on justice and equality for all.[38] Men and women shared equally in leadership roles, and everyone shared in the responsibilities of life together. The Shakers knew that the commitment to share in community was costly, but with it came the gift of simplicity and freedom to be the body of Christ in the world. To value simplicity of life was not just to question values in terms of wealth and prosperity, but it was to throw aside categories which keep people from being one with God and with one another. It was to believe that the categories of rich and poor, young and old, success and failure did not reflect life in God.

The Shakers' emphasis on simplicity of life and communal living echoes many themes that had developed within the monastic tradition of the Church – in particular, the emphasis on a simplicity, chastity and obedience as well as the belief that the day was spent in prayer and work (*ora et labora*). By giving oneself to God in all activities, it was believed that eventually prayer became work and work a prayer, being one and the same: a gift and offering to God. Brother Lawrence (1605–91), a lay brother among the Carmelite order in the seventeenth century who worked in a kitchen of the monastery in France, described this way of life as 'practising the presence of God'. In living in this way, he wrote: 'the time of business does not with me differ from the time of prayer; and in the noise and clatter of my kitchen, while several persons are at the same time calling for different things, I possess God in as great tranquillity as if I were on my knees at the blessed sacrament'.[39]

By putting side by side the two seemingly different expressions of Christian spirituality (the Shakers and the Carmelites) which share certain concerns and longings, we are starkly reminded of the unity found in desire for God which is discovered in diversity in the Church. Today, it is possible to identify many different expressions of ecclesiology or patterns of being the Church. These range from those who in worship want to shout and claim to have ecstatic utterances to those who feel that they must keep silence. It includes highly liturgical services and others that appear to have very little structure at all. It includes communities that are formed around a hierarchical structure of church organization to those who seem to have very little formal leadership at all. There are also patterns of Church which accept the Church joining hands with secular government and those who feel that the Church is best represented as a community that has been 'gathered' or drawn together by God.[40] My purpose here is not to suggest that one model takes precedence over another, but to highlight the fact that every pattern of church life will help to shape and form our understanding of what it means to be in relationship with God and others.

There are, of course, other types of community which, though not ecclesial in nature, may help the Church in its thinking about relatedness and belonging. Some of these have a vision for life together which is informed by Christian faith but they do not claim to be a church and do not demand conformity to a particular kind of doctrinal expression as an essential part of membership with the community. These communities may not claim to be a church community but they have grown out of an understanding of the presence of Christ enabling communion between individuals. This kind of community is exemplified in L'Arche: a network of communities which provide a place for able-bodied and disabled to live together.

Inclusive community: a vision of diversity and difference

Founded by Jean Vanier, in France in 1964, L'Arche communities claim that their purpose is as follows:

1 The aim of L'Arche is to create communities which welcome people with learning disabilities. By this means L'Arche seeks to respond to

the distress of those who are too often rejected, and to give them a valid place in society.

2 L'Arche seeks to reveal the particular gifts of people with learning disabilities who belong at the very heart of their communities and who call others to share their lives.

3 L'Arche knows that it cannot welcome everyone who has a learning disability. It seeks to offer not a solution but a sign, a sign that a society, to be truly human, must be founded on welcome and respect for the weak and downtrodden.

4 In a divided world, L'Arche wants to be a sign of hope. Its communities, founded on covenant relationships between people of differing intellectual capacity, social origin, religion and culture, seek to be a sign of unity, faithfulness and reconciliation.[41]

The movement has grown from the foundation of the first community when Jean Vanier, and Father Thomas Philippe, a Dominican, invited two men with disabilities, Raphael Simi and Philippe Seux, to come and share their lives together in Trosly-Breuil. Having first met Raphael and Philippe in an institution, Vanier and Father Thomas believed that a warm and loving home would have a significant impact on their lives. Their aim was to create a home with them in the spirit of the Gospels, drawing particularly on the beatitudes. With that desire, but no formal knowledge of people with disabilities or training, Vanier, Father Thomas, Raphael and Philippe began their journey together.[42] Soon they all learned that the impact of sharing life together in a simple way had a mutual and significant impact on each of them – what Vanier would later describe as a transformation of the heart.

Today, there are over 110 L'Arche communities in 30 countries throughout the world.[43] Yet, while L'Arche, founded on Christian principles, is not a church, there are many insights into community which may be discovered and drawn from the L'Arche experience. Central to these communities is the emphasis on the value of people and the importance of relationship. Vanier wrote:

> In L'Arche communities we experience that deep inner healing comes about mainly when people feel loved, when they have a sense of belonging. Our communities are essentially places where people can serve and create, and, most importantly, where they can love as well as be loved. This healing flows from relationships – is not something automatic.[44]

Vanier insists that relationship which is based on trust, not coercion or manipulation, is a basic human need.

You see, we were born – we were conceived for communion. And communion is a to and fro of love. Not fusion where I possess you and our frontiers break down and we don't know who we are. Communion is you are you and I am I and we're called to be in communion together – to be one body.[45]

In addition to an emphasis on relationship, L'Arche stresses that community is established on the belief that love is at the heart of communion. Vanier put it this way:

And communion, not fusion, not manipulation, not people domineering no, but communion. I am I and you are you and we can love each other. And to love someone is not . . . it's not sentimentality, it's not emotional stuff, it's to reveal to the other person their beauty. It's to reveal to the other person that they have light inside of them, that they are living beings. And living beings are part of this incredibly beautiful universe of ours. So communion – to be in communion with people is to really love them and to be united, to be one. But we've all been broken, we've been broken.[46]

This emphasis on love at the heart of all communion is also at the heart of Christian spirituality. Relationship has its beginning in love. We love, the Bible says, because God first loved us. Love is at the heart of it. There are moments when we want to turn away, but Christian faith teaches that love compels us to go on loving. Love endures. Love never ends. This love of course is not something we may generate for ourselves, rather Christians understand that it comes from the deep at-oneness with a God who suffered. God who is love holds us together.

Another important feature of community life which is exhibited in L'Arche is related to the issue of power, authority and leadership. A few years ago, one of my students shared with me her experience of living in L'Arche community and claimed that what she now missed the most was 'waiting' in community. 'We always had time', she said. 'If we went on a walk, the slowest was put at the front of the line to lead us. If we ate a meal, everyone waited until the last one had finished.' Her comment reflected the fact that the rhythm of community life in L'Arche communities is established by those who appear to be the weakest. Real communion is based on openness and vulnerability and a recognition of weakness. Vanier claims:

The more community deepens, the weaker and the more sensitive its members become . . . Love makes us weak and vulnerable, because it breaks down the barriers and protective armour we build around ourselves. Love means letting others reach us and becoming sensitive enough to reach them. The cement of unity is interdependence.[47]

Vanier's vision of community is that weakness should be at the heart of every Christian community. Christian faith teaches that at the heart of the community is a cross, a symbol of suffering and death, but likewise a reminder of weakness. 'God chose what was weak in the world', wrote the Apostle Paul, 'to shame the strong' (1 Corinthians 1.27). Yet often the emphasis in the Christian Church is on power and domination. Sadly, the Christian Church has sometimes promoted a religious belief which says that the best people are those who seem successful and who appear self-sufficient, self-confident, all-able, and in-charge. Yet Vanier says that power and cleverness call for admiration but also a certain sense of separation, because we are reminded of what we are not. Community he says is based on radical openness, vulnerability and humility. He wrote:

> Communities are truly communities when they are open to others, when they remain vulnerable and humble; when the members are growing in love, in compassion and in humility. Communities cease to be such when members close in upon themselves with the certitude that they alone have wisdom and truth and expect everyone to be like them and learn from them . . . It is based on forgiveness and openness to those who are different, to the poor and weak . . . Community is the breaking down of barriers to welcome difference.[48]

There is much more which could be said about the patterns of community discovered in the vision of L'Arche. Vanier claims that from 1964 when L'Arche began, he was brought into a world of simple relationships. Through these relationships, he says he was brought into a deeper sense of communion, which is not based on intellectual or abstract conversation, but in simple presence. Vanier's vision of community grounded in love, openness, mutual acceptance, and weakness is based on his own deeply held Christian beliefs. In listening to his story and the story of L'Arche, in the light of the Gospel stories, one may sense the way the story of Christ has shaped his view of community. For instance, when Jesus told his disciples about his journey to the cross, he said that he was going to Jerusalem where he would be mocked, scourged and spat upon before being killed and after three days he would arise. Then, as they were going along the road, his disciples were talking among themselves about who was the greatest. Jesus reminded them that whoever wants to be first must be last of all and servant of all. Then he put a child among them and taking the child in his arms he said 'whoever welcomes one such child in my name welcomes me, and whoever welcomes me welcomes not me but the one who sent me' (Mark 9.30–37).

The picture is one of weakness and vulnerability. The Bible knows nothing of building communities of greatness. Nor is it about gathering together like-minded strong individuals. Rather, as we have seen, community is about diversity and difference as much as sameness or similarity. And also it is about the strength discovered in the weakness and suffering of the cross.

The loss of community

For those who are seeking to understand Christian spirituality, it is important to remember that the longing for relationship or community – while recognized as an integral part of Christian spirituality – is not always interwoven into the patterns of church life. The threads of relationship in the Church have been plucked at and removed for a number of different reasons. A consumer mentality has encouraged many people to treat Christian community as a matter of personal choice rather than a community of calling. Based on a business model of organization, the purpose-driven consumer approach to Christian faith stresses success and satisfaction, and often approaches church life in ways that reflect more of corporate management techniques than community values. Likewise, in some places, Christian faith has been replaced by civil religion which confuses Christian belief with patriotism and loyalty to country and at times encourages Christians to equate cultural or societal values with 'kingdom values'. Both the business model and the approach of civil religion militate against real community because they place very little emphasis on radical openness and vulnerability necessary for the formation of deep and lasting relationship. These models, which are often embraced today as popular expressions of Christian faith, tend to stress power and domination; the strong and not the weak.

Loss of community within the Christian Church may also be the result of too much stress on an institutional framework. One need only look back through the history of the Church to find where the prophetic and transforming work of the Spirit has been hindered by the shackles of a rigid institutional framework. Many if not most prophetic movements within the Church are quickly brought under the control of an institution. This can be seen, for instance, in the development of some of the monastic movements which began as spontaneous vibrant responses to God, but eventually developed patterns and orders which shaped the institutional life. One example of this, of course, is the Franciscan Order which was founded in 1209 by St Francis of Assisi (1181–1226). St Francis' faith was characterized by a joyful response to the gospel which led to a life of poverty and the total renunciation of all material goods for the sake of Christ. The Franciscan order was based on the same ideals, but as the order grew and developed and there was a need for settled communities, it seemed impossible to maintain a strict interpretation of the rule of poverty. This led to disagreement within the order itself which from 1245 onwards led to disputes which were at times quite bitter, threatening the unity of the order as some insisted on a stricter interpretation of the rule than others.

Order is not in itself a bad thing, and perhaps it might be argued that any movement, if it is to thrive, must develop regular patterns and routines for life together. Individuals cannot live in the utter chaos of continuous change and flux, and communities, too, need some pattern or framework. However, the Church sometimes develops a tendency to confuse loyalty to patterns of organization or a framework of doctrine with commitment to Christ and relationship to others within the body of Christ. When this happens people become bound by rules and regulations and may forget that followers of Christ are bound by relationship to Christ and to other members of the body.

In his book, *Christianity in the 21st Century*, sociologist Robert Wuthnow offers further reasons for the loss of community in the Church. Building on the work of Robert Bellah and drawing on the seminal ideas of Hans-Georg Gadamer and Alasdair MacIntyre, Wuthnow suggests that tradition has an important part to play in establishing identity. He asserts that the Church is needed to function as a 'community of memory'. By this, he means that the Church needs to tell stories of the past and help preserve the past. This is not as simple as it might seem at first, due to the fact that many try to retell the past in a way that memorializes or sanitizes history. Sometimes the particular institutional setting a person currently inhabits or tradition which has shaped a person will dictate the way the story is interpreted and told. Yet Wuthnow claims 'the likelihood of anyone in the future retaining the identity of Christian' depends on the telling of stories.[49] Wuthnow is clear that he is not speaking of storytelling that simply reverts to triumphalism. Rather, in agreement with Stanley Hauerwas, Wuthnow suggests that the Church must be a 'community of moral discourse'.[50] That is to say, the stories should reflect the ongoing commitment to Christ that has been a part of Christianity across the generations.

There are many rich sources we could draw from to help us reflect more deeply on this commitment found within Christian community.

One such example is found in a powerful reflection on *Life Together*, in which Dietrich Bonhoeffer, who later died in a Nazi prison camp, rightly claimed that there is a very real difference between community as a human reality and as a spiritual reality. The Church must not simply tell stories which seem to point to a community of our own making. Bonhoeffer claimed that relationship in and through Christ is not an ideal which we must realize, but a reality created by God in Christ in which we may participate.[51] This reality, of course, is a privilege and a grace not to be associated with a right or a demand. Clearly it is something to be discovered and it may be glimpsed when people least expect it – not necessarily at the planned event or programme which is intended to bring people together, but the unexpected encounter with a stranger.

I had just such a chance meeting a few years ago. My husband and I and our children had stopped in a church at Minchinhampton, a small village in the Cotswolds. We were looking around the Church as a few people began to gather for the service of evensong. We had not planned to stay for the service. Our children were at the ages where they were more interested in hearing the echo of their own voices in the Church than the carefully intoned prayers of the vicar. As we began to make our way to the back of the Church, we were stopped by a woman in African dress. She greeted us and there was something in the way she spoke which exuded a deep warmth. It is difficult to explain now, but in an instant, and without words, we sensed that somehow we were all held in a love and by a grace that was greater than ourselves or the tradition of the Church we were standing in. Without hesitation, the woman picked up our young children and gathering each one in turn in her arms, she hugged them and offered a blessing. And with that we went on our way. It was only an unplanned meeting, but there was some deep connectedness, some understanding of community which neither my husband nor I will ever forget.

This story is not told to somehow sentimentalize the Christian understanding of relationship 'in Christ'. However, what I do want to suggest is that bonds of kinship may be experienced at different levels. Two strangers meeting may have little in common, but united in the reality of Christ they have everything in common. This was a bond or union: a communion in Christ. Likewise, it is possible to attend the same church for 20 years and never once know the intimacy of relationship I have described. The point is that this union in Christ is not simply getting to know someone on a human level but is about being bound by God's love at a very different level.

In his book, *Reaching Out: The Three Movements of the Spiritual Life*, a twentieth-century writer, Henri Nouwen, described the movements as:

1) from loneliness to solitude 2) from hostility to hospitality 3) from illusion to prayer. Describing human beings as those who are desperately lonely, while living in the midst of strangers, he stresses the need to discover solitude of the heart. Having done that, he suggests that people can move into relationship with God and others in new ways. The movement into new ways of relating is, according to Nouwen, nothing less than a move from hostility to hospitality. By hospitality, Nouwen means more than simply welcoming a stranger into our homes. He speaks of hospitality as a 'fundamental attitude towards our fellow human beings' which takes the form of creating space where strangers can cast off their strangeness and become fellow human beings. Nouwen suggested that this concept of hospitality can offer a new dimension to our understanding of a healing relationship and the formation of a re-creative community in a world so visibly suffering from alienation and estrangement.[52]

As Nouwen points out, the experience of hospitality in terms of the creation of a free and friendly space where strangers can become friends can happen in many different contexts and at many levels in relationship. One of the examples of the kind of space that can be created is the relationship between students and teachers. Nouwen suggests that in many ways the educational system in most places tends to set up situations where the student and teacher are not present to each other, but in opposition. The teacher, he suggests, is seen as the person who is making demands on the student and the student must meet the demands or fail. Nouwen suggests that the attitude of hospitality would allow for the creation of a place where the student and teacher can 'learn to be present to each other, not as opponents but as those who share in the same struggle in the search for the same truth'.[53] This idea of creating space both to 'be' and to 'become' seems an important aspect of Christian community. Of course, unlike my encounter at Minchinhampton, the space is not created in an instant. Often it takes quite some time to build up the kind of trust necessary for real communion to take place.

The third movement of the spiritual life, according to Nouwen, is from 'illusion to prayer'. Nouwen describes many obstacles which keep us from experiencing relationship with God through prayer and argues that only by casting off our illusions of immortality and giving ourselves to a life of prayer within community will we discover true relationship in God. Of course, Nouwen, like other Christian writers, realized that while we may acknowledge a need for relationship, it takes 'courage to reach out far beyond the limitations of our fragile and finite existence' towards a loving God.[54] Perhaps this is why in the Letter to the Ephesians, there is a prayer for the believers that:

according to the riches of his glory, he may grant that you may be strengthened in your inner being with power through his Spirit, and that Christ may dwell in your hearts through faith, as you are being rooted and grounded in love. I pray that you may have the power to comprehend, with all the saints, what is the breadth and length and height and depth, and to know the love of Christ that surpasses knowledge, so that you may be filled with all the fullness of God. Now to him who by the power at work within us is able to accomplish abundantly far more than all we can ask or imagine, to him be glory in the Church and in Christ Jesus to all generations, forever and ever. Amen (Ephesians 3.14–21).

Significantly, this prayer is not offered for people who have formed the perfect community of faith, but for those who are seeking to understand what it means to 'grow up in every way' into Christ and to be the body of Christ built up in love (Ephesians 4.15–16). It is a prayer for those who are still seeking the way of Christ.

Draw your own conclusions

Think about diversity and difference in community. If genuine Christian community is built around diversity and difference in God, what will it look like?

What is the difference between a community built around a common creed and a community built on the experience of diversity and difference within deep relationship?

How might 'hospitality' be expressed in Christian spirituality?

Dietrich Bonhoeffer wrote: 'Let the one who cannot be alone beware of community.' 'Let the one who is not in community beware of being alone.'[55] What do you think he meant? How might this relate to Christian spirituality?

Further reading

Readings on God as Trinity

Gavin D'Costa (2000), *Sexing the Trinity: Gender Culture and the Divine*, London: SCM Press.
David S. Cunningham (1998), *These Three Are One: The Practice of Trinitarian Theology*, Oxford: Blackwell.
Paul S. Fiddes (2000), *Participating in God: A Pastoral Doctrine of the Trinity*, London: Darton, Longman & Todd.

Miroslav Volf (1998), *After Our Likeness: Church as the Image of the Trinity*, Los Angeles: William Eerdmans.

Readings on community and relationship

Robert N. Bellah *et al.* (1985), *Habits of the Heart: Individualism and Commitment in American Life*, Berkeley, CA: University of California Press.

Jurjen Beumer (1998), *Henri Nouwen, A Restless Seeking for God*, New York: Crossroad.

Robert Durback (ed.) (1989), *Seeds of Hope*, [An anthology of some of Nouwen's writings] London: Darton, Longman & Todd.

Jean Leclerc OSB (1978), *The Love of Learning and the Desire for God: A Study of Monastic Culture*, London: SPCK.

Alistair I. McFayden (1990), *The Call to Personhood: A Christian Theory of the Individual in Social Relationships*, Cambridge: Cambridge University Press.

Henri J.M. Nouwen (1994), *The Return of the Prodigal Son: A Story of Homecoming*, London: Darton, Longman & Todd.

Henri J. M. Nouwen (1995), *The Genesee Diary: Report from a Trappist Monastery*, London: Darton, Longman & Todd.

Norman Shanks (1999), *Iona – God's Energy: The Vision and Spirituality of the Iona Community*, London: Hodder and Stoughton.

Jean Vanier (1976/1993), *Be Not Afraid*, Dublin: Gill and Macmillan.

Jean Vanier (1996 revised edn), *Community and Growth*, London: Darton, Longman & Todd.

Jean Vanier (1999), *Becoming Human*, London: Darton, Longman & Todd.

Miroslav Volf (1996), *Exclusion and Embrace: A Theological Exploration of Identity, Otherness, and Reconciliation*, Nashville: Abingdon Press.

Walter Wink (1984), *Naming the Powers: The Language of Power in the New Testament*, Philadelphia: Fortress Press.

Walter Wink (1986), *Unmasking the Powers: The Invisible Forces that Determine Human Existence*, Philadelphia: Fortress Press.

Walter Wink (1992), *Engaging the Powers*, Minneapolis: Augsburg/Fortress Press.

Walter Wink (1999), *The Powers that Be: Theology for A New Millennium*, New York: Doubleday.

Readings on the Orthodox Church

John Chryssavgis (2004), *Light Through Darkness: The Orthodox Tradition*, London: Darton, Longman & Todd.

Timothy Ware (1963/1984), *The Orthodox Church*, Harmondsworth: Penguin Books.

Readings on ecumenism

Ellen Flesseman-van Leer (1983), *The Bible, Its Authority and Interpretation in the Ecumenical Movement*, Geneva: WCC Publications.

Jeffrey Gros FSC, Harding Meyer and Willaim G. Rusch (eds) (2000), *Growth in Agreement II, Reports and Agreed Statements of Ecumenical Conversations on a World Level, 1982–1998*, Geneva: WCC Publications.

Diane Kessler and Michael Kinnamon, *Council of Churches and the Ecumenical Vision*, Geneva: WCC Publications.

Michael Kinnamon and Brian E. Cope (eds) (1997), *The Ecumenical Movement: An Anthology of Key Texts and Voices*, Geneva: WCC Publications.

Geoffrey Wainwright (1983), *The Ecumenical Movement*, Grand Rapids: William Eerdmans.

Notes

1 David McMillan and David M. Chavis (1976), 'Sense of Community: A Definition and Theory', *Journal of Community Psychology*, Vol. 14 (January), pp. 6–23.

2 Wendell Berry (2004), *Hannah Coulter*, Emeryville, CA: Shoemaker & Hoard, pp. 93–4.

3 Berry, *Hannah Coulter*, p. 113.

4 Stanley Hauerwas (1989), 'The Servant Community Christian Social Ethic', in John Berkman and Michael Cartwright (eds) (2001), *The Hauerwas Reader*, Durham, N.C. and London: Duke University Press, p. 371.

5 Thomas Merton (1968), *Zen and The Birds of Appetite*, New York: New Directions, p. 39.

6 Thomas Merton (1968), *Conjectures of a Guilty Bystander*, Garden City New York: Image/Doubleday, pp. 156–7.

7 Mark Gibbard (1974), *Twentieth-Century Men of Prayer*, London: SCM Press, pp. 71–2.

8 John O'Donohue (1998/2000), *Eternal Echoes*, London: Bantam Press, p. 372.

9 St Patrick, 'A Prayer', in *The Oxford Book of Prayer* (1985), Oxford: Oxford University Press, p. 129.

10 M. A. Seifrid (1993), 'In Christ', in *Dictionary of Paul and His Letters*, ed. Gerald F. Hawthorne, Ralph P. Martin and Daniel G. Reid, Downers Grove, Ill.: Inter-Varsity Press, pp. 433–6.

11 Miroslav Volf (1998), *After Our Likeness: The Church as the Image of the Trinity*, Grand Rapids: William Eerdmans, p. 2.

12 Volf, *After Our Likeness*, pp. 18ff.

13 Colin Gunton (1997), *The Promise of Trinitarian Theology*, Edinburgh: T&T Clark, p. 80.

14 Gunton, *Trinitarian Theology*, p. 80.

15 Gunton, *Trinitarian Theology*, p. 81.

16 Paul S. Fiddes (2000), *Participating in God: A Pastoral Doctrine of the Trinity*, London: Darton, Longman & Todd, p. 72.

17 Fiddes, *Participating in God*, p. 72.

18 In the third and fourth centuries, theologians in the East and West debated the way one understands the idea that God is 'one essence, three persons'. For a survey of the issues surrounding the debate, see Fiddes, *Participating in God*, pp. 13ff.

19 David Cunningham (1998), *These Three Are One*, Oxford: Blackwell, p. 211.

20 Cunningham, *These Three Are One,* p. 165.

21 Cunningham, *These Three Are One,* p. 165.

22 For a helpful discussion of some of these matters, see Fiddes, *Participating in God*, pp. 11–61.

23 Henry Chadwick (1967), *The Early Church*, Harmondsworth: Penguin Books, p. 84.

24 Chadwick, *The Early Church*, p. 84.

25 This phrase is borrowed from a book by Jeffrey Burton Russell (1968), *A History of Medieval Christianity: Prophecy and Order*, Arlington Heights, Ill.: Harlon Davidson.

26 H. Richard Niebuhr (1951), *Christ and Culture*, New York: Harper & Row, pp. 83ff.; Geoffrey Wainwright, 'Types of Spirituality', in Cheslyn Jones, Geoffrey Wainwright, Edward Yarnold, S.J. (1986), *The Study of Spirituality*, London: SPCK, pp. 592–605.

27 World Council of Churches website, http://wcc-coe.org/wcc/who/cuv-e.html, accessed 14 March 2007.

28 World Council of Churches website, http://wcc-coe.org/wcc/who/cuv-e.html.

29 Michael Kinnamon (1988), *Truth and Community: Diversity and Its Limits in the Ecumenical Movement*, Grand Rapids: William Eerdmans, p. 18.

30 Kinnamon, *Truth and Community*, p. 18.

31 Austin Flannery (1975), *Vatican Council II: The Conciliar and Post-Conciliar Documents*, Collegeville, MN.: Liturgical Press, pp. 350–440.

32 Hans Küng (1982), *The Church Maintained in Truth*, New York: Vintage Books, p. 11.

33 Kathryn Spink (1986), *A Universal Heart: The Life and Vision of Brother Roger of Taizé*, London: SPCK.

34 R. Schutz (1968), *Violent for Peace*, London: Darton, Longman & Todd, p. 49.

35 Information from Taizé website http://www.taize.fr/en, accessed 14 May 2007.

36 Chadwick, *The Early Church*, p. 220.

37 Edward Deming Andrews (1940), *The Gift to Be Simple: Songs, Dances and Rituals of the American Quakers*, New York: Dover, p. 136.

38 R. E. Whiston (1983), *The Shakers: Two Centuries of Spiritual Reflection*, Classics of Western Spirituality, London: SPCK, p. 203.

39 Brother Lawrence (1968), *Practicing the Presence of God, being Conversations and Letters of Nicholas Herman of Lorraine*, Westwood N.J.: Fleming H. Revell, pp. 30–1.

40 The congregational way held that the Church is a *society* or *fellowship* of believers who profess to give themselves to the Lord and to one another and join together with Scripture as a guide to faith and practice. See Ernest Payne (1952), *The Fellowship of Believers*, London: Carey Kingsgate Press.

41 L'Arche community website at http://www.larche.org.uk/, accessed 14 March 2007.

42 Kathryn Spink (1990), *Jean Vanier and L'Arche, A Communion of Love*, London: Darton, Longman & Todd, p. 40.

43 Jean Vanier (1999), *Becoming Human*, London: Darton, Longman & Todd, p. 6.

44 Vanier, *Becoming Human*, p. 11.

45 Interview with Jean Vanier, David Cherniack Films, Canadian Broadcast corporation http://ca.geocities.com/dcherniack@rogers.com/vanier.htm, accessed 14 March 2007.

46 Interview at http://ca.geocities.com/dcherniack@rogers.com/vanier.htm, accessed 14 March 2007.

47 Jean Vanier (1979), *Community and Growth*, London: Darton, Longman & Todd, p. 48.

48 Vanier, *Community and Growth*, pp. 19–20.

49 Robert Wuthnow (1993), *Christianity in the 21st Century*, Oxford: Oxford University Press, p. 48.

50 Wuthnow, *Christianity*, p. 49.

51 Dietrich Bonhoeffer (1954), *Life Together*, San Francisco: Harper & Row, p. 26.

52 Henri Nouwen (1976/1983), *Reaching Out, The Three Movements of the Spiritual Life*, Glasgow: Collins, Fount Paperbacks, pp. 63ff.

53 Nouwen, *Reaching Out*, p. 80.

54 Nouwen, *Reaching Out*, p. 105.

55 Bonhoeffer, *Life Together*, p. 11.

4

Searching for the Way of Christ

It was a bright, crisp cold day when I saw him walking on the road. I was heading in a different direction, but something about him caught my attention. He wore baggy trousers and an old coat. On his back he had a pack which appeared to contain all his belongings. He had a bed roll, clothes, pots and pans and a teapot dangling from one side of the pack. I watched the man until he disappeared down the road and found myself wondering about his story. Who was the man? Where had he been? Where was he going? Was he planning to settle? Was he looking for something or someone?

Many years later, I still have the picture of the lone traveller in my mind. I imagine it is because the image identifies the basic nature of longing which is part of all humankind. This sense of search, as we have already noted, can be described in different ways. For some it is a search for peace, light, hope or knowledge. Christians speak of the search as a longing for God. John S. Dunne described it in this way: 'something that went on without ceasing in my life, the restless movement of desire, and I had seen that desire is an unconscious yearning for God.'[1]

The Christian life: a pilgrimage

The idea of making a journey has been used as a metaphor for the whole of the Christian life: its beginning, its process and its goal. Similarly, the language of pilgrimage has also been central to the practice of Christian devotion and is often used in devotional exercises and on retreats. In fact, the focus of the Christian year which begins at Advent, and moves through Christmas, Epiphany, Lent, Easter, and Pentecost is based on the idea of journeying through the Christ story. Moreover, incorporated into each of these seasons, there is often a special emphasis on journey, such as in Lent, the 40-day period before Easter, when many Christians devote themselves to fasting and penitence, which is the period when people think of Jesus' time of testing and temptation for 40 days and 40 nights in the wilderness. At other times of the year, too, as part of Christian devotion, some people find it helpful to make personal pilgrimages to places that are set apart as holy (e.g. Walsingham or Lourdes). Within the history of the Church, such devotional practices are based on the premise that a pilgrimage enables people to recognize where they have been and perhaps to move forward in a step of faith and trust or, alternatively, the pilgrimage is a journey into prayer or perhaps the journey itself becomes a prayer. *The Way of a Pilgrim*, for example, which was written anonymously in the nineteenth century, describes the journey of a Russian Orthodox pilgrim who is seeking to discover how to 'pray without ceasing'. As he travels, he speaks to other people along the way and discovers the value of repeating the 'Jesus prayer': 'Lord Jesus Christ, Son of God, have mercy on me, a sinner.' As the words were repeated over and over, they helped create rhythm of the outward and the inward journey. Jesus became the centre, the heart beat of the pilgrim's life. Today the ancient tradition of repeating short 'centring' prayers continues to be used as a method helping Christians make the inward journey from 'head to heart'.[2]

Central to any purposeful journey is the recognition that there is a beginning and an ending. The traveller has the sense that she is going somewhere or that her search is taking her someplace. In some expressions of Christian spirituality it appears that the main purpose of the journey is to reach the end goal which is described as heaven or paradise. Hence, many hymns and devotional books have conveyed the idea that simply to be ready to attain heavenly rest is the primary purpose of the Christian life. Yet this is an incomplete picture of the Christian life, for in Christian spirituality, the longing is not simply for a place to rest, it is also for a place to be and to become. That means that attention must be given not only to the goal of the journey, but to the process as well.

Beginnings and endings, as well as the shape and form that the journey takes, are often disputed and debated by Christians. Some people, for instance, want to speak of one beginning point, while others believe that it is possible to speak of having many new beginnings as an individual discovers God's love in fresh and unexpected ways. Moreover, while some would want to chart progress on the journey very carefully with set periods of self-reflection and rigorous disciplines of devotion, others would argue that progress on the journey is often not realized until the traveller moves on some distance and then stops and looks back. Most Christians would agree, however, that at some point on the journey there is often a sense of a new beginning or a new orientation which comes from a decision to turn around (repentance) in response to God's love and receiving God's free gift of acceptance (grace). Then in the freedom of forgiveness, a person embarks on a journey with God and for God and, in some sense, to God as well. It is a journey of hope and promise perhaps more than one of clarity of vision. For the Bible says that is what faith is: 'the assurance of things hoped for, the conviction of things unseen' (Hebrews 11.1).

The beginning and the in-between: conversion and calling

This idea of searching for the way of Christ has been depicted in many different devotional works, among them, the well-known seventeenth-century allegory by John Bunyan, *Pilgrim's Progress*. Bunyan describes Christian making a journey in order to present his particular understanding of the plan of salvation. Christian, dressed in rags, with a burden on his back and a book in his hand faces away from his house. He leaves the City of Destruction and goes in search of the Heavenly City. Ultimately he reaches his destination, though all along the way he faces great trials and difficulties. At one point, for instance, after a night of difficulty, Christian looks back at the trials he had faced in the darkness:

> Now morning being come he looked back, not of desire to return, but to see by the light of the day what hazards he had gone through in the dark. So he saw more perfectly the ditch that was on the one hand, and the quag that was on the other; also how narrow the way was which lay betwixt them both; also now he saw hobgoblins, and satyrs, and dragons of the pit, but all afar off; for after break of day they came not nigh; yet they were discovered to him, according to that which is written: He discovereth deep things out of darkness, and bringeth out to light the shadow of death.[3]

Often viewed as an allegory of the Christian life, the narrative relating Pilgrim's safe passage through the trials and travails of life was seen as an encouragement to others to remain resolute in their commitment to the Way of Christ. Gordon Mursell suggests that Bunyan depicted this idea of pilgrimage as a thrilling adventure to the call of God. The adventure, however, claims Mursell, 'is not an option: all of us must embark upon it . . . because it is part of what it means to be human'.[4]

When thinking of Christian spirituality, of course, it is not enough to say that the sense of search is simply 'part of what it means to be human'. As noted in Chapter 1, the search is not simply about an individual longing for God, but equally, in Christian spirituality, the search is about an individual responding to the longing of God. Christians describe their response in different ways. Sometimes, they speak of their response to God as a moment of conversion. Others would reflect on a series of events which led them to a moment in which they turned away from an old life in repentance and turned to God in faith and trust. Many would claim that this experience should be followed by baptism (and/or confirmation) and membership in the Church of Christ.

Other Christians believe conversion is a process. They might describe a very long period in which they slowly began to turn in response to God. For some, this would begin with having been baptized as an infant and received into the Church and followed later by a response to Christ expressed publicly through the rite of confirmation. For others it might reflect a decision made after being brought up in another faith tradition or in none at all. However one views the initial step, most Christians want to claim that there is a starting point; a time when one recognizes the beginning of a life with God and for God. This idea of conversion, however, is not necessarily a momentary event. While some Christians like to refer to the day they 'were saved' others feel it better to speak of the process whereby they are 'being saved'. Both ideas may be found in the New Testament. In fact, the New Testament speaks of salvation in terms of a past, present and future event.[5] The important point for most Christians is that God has taken the initiative by continually reaching out in love to humankind and, indeed, to all creation. Having taken the initiative in love, God as Creator waits and longs for creation's response of love. In one sense perhaps this is what salvation (understood also as healing and wholeness) is about; the idea that one is continually being changed or drawn closer by love in order to love.

In Christian spirituality, the idea of conversion, even as a lifelong, on-going process of salvation, is not the only way of speaking of responding to God's longing love. In addition to the idea of being changed, by God's grace, into the likeness of Christ, (converted) Christians also sometimes refer to being 'called' by God. For Christians, God 'calling' a person is closely associated with the idea of vocation (Latin *vocare* – to call) and often has been used to speak of a sense that one has had a divine call to a particular career or occupation. Sometimes people think of Christian ministers or priests as being 'called' to a special office or at least called out to a special ministry of preaching, teaching, pastoral care, etc. Yet in the Christian tradition there is also the sense that others, too, are 'called' to serve Christ, which might include a long-term vocation or simply refer to a response to a person or an event. A person might claim to be 'called' to some specific task in a community of faith, such as serving tea after a worship service, helping with a parent and toddler group or assisting with a Fair Trade project. On the other hand, a person may describe his or her job not in terms of a secular employment, but as a 'calling' (e.g. in nursing or medicine).

The notion of calling is expressed in many different ways in the Bible. In the widest sense of the word, every Christian is believed to be called by God: first, to respond in faith and trust to God's gracious gift of love to us, but in a deeper sense to serve Christ as Lord. In the Old and New Testaments, there are many stories about God calling people. In these biblical narratives, 'calling' is often depicted in a very personal and specific way. Moses, for example, felt called to lead the Israelites out of Egypt (Exodus 3.1–12). Jesus called men and women to follow him (Matthew 4.18–21; Luke 8.1–3). The Apostle Paul claimed that he heard the risen Christ speaking to him on the road to Damascus as he found himself called to proclaim the gospel of Jesus Christ (Acts 22.6–16).

The Christian spiritual writings include both stories about 'conversion' as well as stories about a 'calling' to a task. Sometimes the two seem inseparable. That is to say that the calling to a task is also in some way a response to 'someone' or 'something'. Dag Hammarskjöld, the Secretary-General of the United Nations from 1953 to 1961, wrote of a clear sense of calling, though he was not sure when, how, or from whom he received the call. As he described it:

> I don't know Who – or what – put the question, I don't know when it was put. I don't even remember answering. But at some moment I did answer Yes to Someone – or Something – and from that hour I was certain that existence is meaningful and that, therefore, my life, in self-surrender, had a goal. From that moment I have known what it means 'not to look back', and 'to take no thought for the morrow'.[6]

In reading passages such as this one from Hammarskjöld's diary, which was published posthumously in 1963 under the title *Markings*, it is evident that he was nurtured by Scripture as well as by reading works of the Christian mystics. However, it does not appear that Hammarskjöld worshipped regularly with a particular church community and he rarely spoke of his faith. In fact, when his journal was published some people expressed surprise because they had not realized that he had embraced Christian faith. Yet, while he did not describe his Christian experience in the way that others might expect, Hammarskjöld's reflections on his experience are a reminder that the expressions of conversion and calling are vast and myriad. While there have been attempts in the past by some Christians to suggest that conversion should follow a particular pattern (acknowledgement of sin, conviction, submission, fear, sorrow and faith) the witness of the Christian tradition is that the longing love of God meets the longing of individuals in surprising and often unexpected ways.[7]

Simone Weil, a French writer who grew up in a Jewish family in the early part of the twentieth century, claimed that she experienced the presence of Christ when a poem she had memorized became her prayer. She wrote:

> I discovered the poem . . . called 'Love'. I learnt it by heart. Often . . .
> I make myself say it over, concentrating all my attention upon it, and
> clinging with all my soul to the tenderness it enshrines. I used to think
> I was merely reciting it as a beautiful poem, but without my knowing
> it the recitation had the virtue of a prayer. It was during one of these
> recitations that, as I told you, Christ himself came down and took pos-
> session of me . . .
> Until last September I had never once prayed in all my life.[8]

The 'Love' poem which Weil refers to was written by the seventeenth-century English writer and pastor, George Herbert, and it depicts the way God's love calls and beckons a person.

> Love bade me welcome: yet my soul drew back,
>   Guilty of dust and sin.
> But quick-ey'd Love, observing me grow slack
>   From my first entrance in,
> Drew nearer to me, sweetly questioning
>   If I lack'd any thing.
> 'A guest', I answer'd, 'worthy to be here':
>   Love said, 'you shall be he.'
> 'I the unkind, ungrateful: Ah, my dear,
>   I cannot look on thee.'
> Love took my hand, and smiling did reply,
>   'Who made the eyes but I?'
> 'Truth Lord, but I have marr'd them: let my shame
>   Go where it doth deserve.'
> 'And know you not, says Love, who bore the blame?'
>   'My dear, then I will serve.'
> 'You must sit down', says Love, 'and taste my meat':
>   So I did sit and eat.[9]

Weil felt that she had been beckoned, 'called' by God, though she claimed that she had never before thought about God in terms of relationship.

In my arguments about the insolubility of the problem of God I had never foreseen the possibility of that, of a real contact, person to person, here below, between a human being and God. I had vaguely heard tell of things of this kind, but I had never believed in them. In the Fioretti the accounts of apparitions rather put me off if anything, like the miracles in the Gospel. Moreover, in this sudden possession of me by Christ, neither my senses nor my imagination had any part; I only felt in the midst of my suffering the presence of a love, like that which one can read in the smile on a beloved face.[10]

Like Hammarskjöld, Weil was never a member of a traditional Christian community. In fact, she was never baptized. Yet there can be no doubt from her reflections that she thought deeply about the love of God demonstrated in the death of Christ on the cross and had committed herself to journey toward and with this God of love who possessed her. She wrote:

God created through love and for love. God did not create anything except love itself, and the means to love. He created love in all its forms. He created beings capable of love from all possible distances. Because no other could do it, he himself went to the greatest possible distance, the infinite distance. This infinite distance between God and God, this supreme tearing apart, this agony beyond all others, this marvel of love, is the crucifixion. Nothing can be further from God than that which has been made accursed.

This tearing apart, over which supreme love places the bond of supreme union, echoes perpetually across the universe in the midst of the silence, like two notes, separate yet melting into one, like pure and heart-rending harmony. This is the Word of God. The whole creation is nothing but its vibration. When human music in its greatest purity pierces our soul, this is what we grasp more distinctly through it.

Those who persevere in love hear this note from the lowest depths into which affliction has thrust them. From that moment they can no longer have any doubt.[11]

In looking at stories of a religious experience of 'call' or 'conversion', what is clear is that there is an infinite variety of ways in which people describe their experience of God. Sometimes the stories, like Hammarskjöld's, are quite matter-of-fact. There is no high drama, no outpouring of emotion and no sense of excitement. Conversely, others leave no doubt that their encounter with God left them feeling overwhelmed. A piece of parchment recording an encounter was found sewn into Blaise Pascal's clothing after his death, and it appears that he carried it with him at all times. It read:

The year of grace 1654,
Monday, 23 November, feast of St Clement,
Pope and Martyr, and of others in the Martyrology.
Eve of St Chrysogonus, Martyr and others.
From about half past ten in the evening until half past midnight,
FIRE
'God of Abraham, God of Isaac, God of Jacob,'
not of philosophers and scholars,
Certainty, certainty, heartfelt, joy, peace.
God of Jesus Christ.
God of Jesus Christ.
'My God and your God,'
'Thy God shall be my God.'
The world forgotten, and everything except God.
He can only be found by the ways taught in the Gospels.
Greatness of the human soul.
'O righteous Father, the world had not known thee, but I have known
    thee.'
Joy, joy, joy, tears of joy.
I have cut myself off from him
'They have forsaken me, the fountain of living waters.'
'My God wilt thou forsake me?'
Let me not be cut off from him for ever!
'And this is life eternal, that they might know thee, the
only true God, and Jesus Christ whom thou has sent.'
Jesus Christ.
Jesus Christ.
I have cut myself off from him, shunned him, denied him, crucified
    him.
Let me never be cut off from him!
He can only be kept by the ways taught in the Gospels.
Sweet and total renunciation.
Total submission to Jesus Christ and my director.
Everlasting joy in return for one day's effort on earth.
I will not forget thy word. Amen.[12]

Pascal seems to be describing an encounter with God that is something akin to a biblical theophany. Yet, his experience of God was not simply an emotional feeling which excluded reason. Pascal was not opposed to thinking about God, but he claimed that to be consistent with reason, one must at times deny reason.[13] As he put it, there were 'two excesses: to exclude reason, to admit nothing but reason'.[14] It seems that Pascal realized what many other Christian writers have tried to express:

> Reason's last step is the recognition that there are an infinite number of things which are beyond it. It is merely feeble if it does not go as far as to realize that.
>
> If natural things are beyond it, what are we to say about supernatural things?[15]

In all the accounts of conversion or calling, it is interesting to note the varied and different ways that people describe their journey of faith. For some it seems to begin with a deeply felt emotional experience, while for others it is a process of intellectual engagement. At times, as the journey unfolds, it may be necessary to move to a different community of faith in order to worship and give expression to faith. Such was the case for John Henry Newman, a leader of the Oxford Movement in the nineteenth century, who left the Church of England and was received into the Roman Catholic Church in 1845. There were a number of political and sociological as well as doctrinal reasons for Newman's abdication from Anglicanism, but when he eventually joined the Roman Catholic Church, he obviously felt he had been making a journey and he claimed later that 'it was like coming into port after a rough sea; and my happiness on that score remains to this day without interruption'.[16]

The journey theme was significant to Newman throughout his Christian life. In 1833, when he was travelling in Italy, he fell ill and had to delay his trip home. When he was finally on board ship returning to England he wrote:

> Lead, kindly Light, amid the encircling gloom, Lead Thou me on;
> The night is dark, and I am far from home; lead Thou me on.
> Keep Thou my feet; I do not ask to see
> The distant scene; one step enough for me.
>
> I was not ever thus, nor prayed that Thou shouldst lead me on;
> I loved to choose and see my path; but now lead Thou me on;
> I loved the garish day, and, spite of fears,
> Pride ruled my will: Remember not past years.

So long Thy power hath blest me, sure it still will lead me on.
O'er moor and fen, o'er crag and torrent, till the night is gone,
And with the morn those angel faces smile, which I
Have loved long since, and lost awhile.[17]

Hymns and songs such as this one have been an important part of Christian spirituality. Music, and particularly hymnody in public worship, has offered Christians an opportunity to give public expression to their personal devotion. Like many other writers, Newman used hymns to highlight important themes in the Christian spiritual tradition, in this instance, the idea of a life of faith being a journey or pilgrimage.

While it is natural to think of the Christian journey in individualistic terms, singing a hymn such as this in worship is yet another reminder that the Christian journey is shared with others. Indeed, as we have seen, we have been made for and live in relationship. The Christian life is made in the context of life with God, others and indeed the wider world. In Bunyan's story of *Pilgrim's Progress*, while Christian may appear to be making the journey alone, in fact, he meets and shares with many companions along the way who offer advice, warning and encouragement.

The journey outward: walking in the world

The emphasis on journey with others is a central theme in any exploration of Christian spirituality and has been taken up in both the Old and New Testaments. In the Old Testament, stories are told of the Israelites making a journey together toward the promised land. They were pilgrims on a journey and they travelled with one another and with God toward the place God had promised them. Similarly, in the New Testament, Jesus' disciples are called to follow him, to be with him, to accompany him to Jerusalem. According to John's Gospel, when Thomas, one of Jesus' disciples, asked how they could know 'the way' in order to follow him, Jesus told his disciples, 'I am the way, the truth, and the life' (John 14.6).

Initially, it seems that the followers of Jesus do not understand the nature of the journey with Jesus. They think they will always be travelling the road with Jesus as he continues to proclaim the news of the coming of God's kingdom. Although he began to teach them that the 'Son of Man' must suffer many things, and be rejected, and killed and after three days arise, they do not seem to grasp that this road of suffering was also the road they were called to travel (Mark 8.31–38). In John's Gospel, the disciples are told specifically by Jesus that 'in a little while' he must go away, but he promises them that they will 'not be left as orphans' but will know the presence of the Advocate, the Holy Spirit (the Paraclete – literally the one who will come alongside) (John 14.15–18). Yet, as the Gospel writers make plain, still they did not understand.

In the New Testament accounts of the events after Jesus' death and resurrection, the Lord appears to his disciples. The risen Christ of the Gospels is one who both comes and meets his followers on a journey and travels with them too. In Luke, for instance, there is the very powerful story of the risen Christ meeting his followers on the road to Emmaus. In the story, he walks with them, explains the Scriptures and then stays with them in order to share a meal, but they do not immediately recognize him. According to Luke, it is not until then that their 'eyes were opened' (Luke 24.13–35).

The journey theme is continued by Luke in Acts, when he describes the way the power of the risen Lord as being made known through other believers. The followers of Jesus are directed toward others who are making a journey and they also meet companions on the road who reveal the love and power of Christ to them. There is, for instance, the story of Philip meeting the Ethiopian official, or Saul on the road to Damascus (Acts 8.26–40; 9.1–19). Significantly, in all these accounts, the idea of journey is used to frame the experience of the disciples. As they make their journey, as they walk the road looking for the way, they encounter the Christ. Finally, it seems that in the New Testament, the followers of Jesus began to understand that they were made for relationship. So their search for God was a search which took place in communal life. The search was not simply for communion, but equally within communion. Their longing was joined with the longing of God and with the longing of others within community.

Nourishment for the journey: worship and the sacraments

In looking at some stories of conversion and calling, Christian faith may seem to be a solitary experience between an individual and God. Yet, as we have already seen, while some experiences of conversion and calling may be intensely personal, Christian spirituality knows nothing of private, individualistic faith. Very early on in the history of the Church, patterns of liturgy and worship emerged which enabled worshippers to give expression to both the personal and corporate nature of faith. For instance, the development of the sacraments (defined as an outward and visible sign of an inward and spiritual grace) in some churches include baptism and the Lord's Supper, while other traditions would add confirmation, marriage, ordination, penance and last rites. The sacraments, which are sometimes seen as ways of nurturing personal individual faith, are also a reminder of the united, corporate nature of it.

Christians have different ways of describing the sacraments and they disagree on their number and nature. Some people believe there are seven sacraments of the Church while others hold to two and still others none. Some view participation in the sacraments as an opportunity for individuals to receive the benefits of God's grace. Others feel that the sacraments are not efficacious for salvation and merely serve as reminders of the immensity of God's love for the whole of creation. Yet, for all Christians who observe the sacraments, both the administration of them and participation in them is a reminder of the mutual sharing in the Church as the Body of Christ. As the Apostle Paul wrote to the Christians in Corinth: 'The cup of blessing that we bless, is it not a sharing in the blood of Christ? The bread we break, is it not a sharing in the body of Christ? Because there is one bread, we who are many are one body, for we all partake of the one bread' (1 Corinthians 10.16–17).

In addition to the sacraments, there are many other elements of worship such as music, prayer, preaching, liturgical and non-liturgical patterns, and different attitudes with regard to architecture, time and place. There is not scope here to discuss the many ways that congregational worship in its varied expressions and patterns nourishes Christian spirituality. Yet within every tradition there is a recognition of the fact that as we journey in worship, we journey with others, both on earth and in heaven.

The journey inward: retreat from the world

The concept of people yearning together for all that God desires does not deny of course that there are moments when individuals must withdraw from the world in order to listen to God. The Gospel writers tell us that there were times when Jesus withdrew to a deserted place to pray. Following this example, many Christians believe that it is necessary to have regular times to withdraw from the activities of the world in order to give themselves to prayer. Sometimes this is done on a daily basis in the form of a time of devotion referred to in some traditions as a 'quiet time'. For others, withdrawal from the world might also take the form of some kind of retreat. This might be for a day or a week or longer. This practice of having regular times and rhythms for prayer was always part of Christian worship and most certainly reflects its Jewish heritage. The emphasis on withdrawal for prayer may reflect the idea among early Christians that they were citizens of two worlds, the heavenly and the earthly. As they struggled to know how they could live in the world and yet not be of it, they focused on the need to give oneself to God in prayer continually.[18] Individuals, as well as the whole community, were to journey in prayer with God. As Joseph Jungmann has put it:

> The church of God is the community of those whom he has called and who answer him in the language of prayer . . . Prayer accompanies the Church on her pilgrimage through this world and will not be silenced till the day of her final consummation.[19]

By the third century, there were both men and women who fled to the Egyptian desert in order to give themselves to God. They became known as the Desert Fathers and Mothers. The outward physical journey they made characteristically began by giving up possessions, in order to focus more fully on God or, perhaps better, to experience 'the abundance of God's presence'.[20]

Following the example of Jesus who went out into the wilderness and was tempted and tested, so they fled to the desert in order to do battle with the powers of evil and give themselves to an inner journey of finding their true self in God. In order to detach themselves from the world, they gave themselves to a disciplined lifestyle that included such things as fasting, prayer vigils, and long periods of solitude. They also practised hospitality and knew how to create space for others who were also making the inner journey to discover being in God.[21]

Our knowledge of the desert tradition comes mainly from the sayings of the Desert Fathers and Mothers which were collected and handed down as a way of encouraging others who were seeking to follow the Christian way. The sayings were often repeated and passed on in the form of a dialogue between two people: a question is posed to an Abba or Amma and they give a reply, usually in the form of a wise saying or story. For instance: 'Abba Poemen said to Abba Joseph: Tell me how I can become a monk. He replied: "If you want to find here and hereafter, say on every occasion, who am I? And do not judge anyone."'[22] This early desert tradition is closely linked with St Antony, who was born in Egypt about AD 251, and is said to have lived a solitary ascetic life in the desert in the third century. *The Life of St Antony*, written by Athanasius in the fourth century, was intended to portray Antony as the ideal monk. He is depicted as a man who took literally the words of the Gospel that 'if you wish to be perfect, go, sell your possessions, and give the money to the poor, and you will have treasure in heaven; then come, follow me' (Matthew 19.21).

Once committed to the solitary life, Antony was determined to fight with the powers that sought to possess him. At one point as he experienced conflict with evil, he cried out 'Where were you Lord while I went through such tribulations?' A voice answered, 'I was here by your side, Antony, I have never left you . . . I will be your guide and comforter.'[23]

Although the desert Ammas and Abbas are sometimes viewed as representatives of that pattern of the Christian way seen as a solitary or individual search, their approach was not in any sense to be understood as in the modern sense a journey of self-discovery. In fact there is an emphasis on sharing with others. The Desert Fathers and Mothers were spiritual guides who made space to listen to others. And eventually some left the desert and went back to join again with others. Athanasius claims, for instance, that after 20 years in the desert, St Antony allowed the door to be broken down by the people and returned with them to the village.

In Christian spirituality, the desert became not so much a literal place, but a symbol of the time and place of testing in the Christian life. Ian Bradley points out that in the Celtic tradition, it symbolized for them a 'perpetual exile and seeking after Christ'.[24] In this way, the wilderness became a powerful symbol of resurrection as well as a place of penance. It is true of course that there are occasions when we may choose to go on pilgrimage to the desert, but at other times we have a wilderness experience forced on us. However it may be experienced, Christians believe that the desert may be a place of growth as individuals do battle with forces that keep a person from drawing near to God. For the Desert Fathers and Mothers, their main weapon for battle was unceasing prayer which in this Eastern tradition was to be simple and direct.

> Abba Macarius, for instance, taught his disciples not to use many words when they prayed; rather they should frequently stretch out their arms saying: 'Lord, as you know best and in the manner you will, have pity on me'; or when in distress: 'Help Me'.[25]

As monasticism developed in the Church, there was a move from the idea of solitary individuals living alone (anchoritic monasticism), to groups of monks being drawn together into community (cenobitic monasticism). Over the years, many monastic communities have formed on the basis of the three-fold vow of poverty, chastity and obedience. As the monastic movements grew and spread, they had a tremendous influence on the

Church and society as they focused on things like education, preaching, care for the poor and the sick and, of course, prayer.

Many of the devotional manuals and books on prayer were written by monks who were seeking to encourage others to give themselves to God in prayer. It is through these monastic writings that some of the approaches to prayer from the eastern church found their way into the west. John Cassian, for example, who was born in the east around AD 360, was greatly influenced by another eastern thinker, Evagrius, through whom he received knowledge of the work of Origen, who was an important Christian thinker.

Cassian wrote two major works (the *Conferences* and the *Institutes*) which were intended to give direction to monks. In these he offers guidance from the eastern tradition on prayer and the monastic life. For him, prayer was to be pure and unceasing. The entire goal of the monk was to move toward continual and uninterrupted prayer. In Conference 1, on prayer, Cassian reminds the reader of the teaching of Abba Isaac and claims that nothing should distract a person from prayer.

> And therefore in order that prayer may be offered up with an earnestness and purity with which it ought to be, we must by all means observe these rules. First all anxiety about carnal things must be entirely got rid of; next we must leave no room for not merely the care but even the recollection of any business affairs, and in like manner must also lay aside all backbitings, vain and incessant chattering, and buffoonery; anger above all . . . there must be laid the secure foundations of a deep humility, which may be able to support a tower that shall reach the sky . . .[26]

This emphasis on prayer, humility and love as essential ingredients in the Christian's life are recurring themes in these monastic writings. In his work, *On the Love of God*, for instance, Bernard of Clairvaux (1090–1153), speaks of the need to learn humility and then advance in love in four stages: 1) love of self for self; 2) love of God for what God gives; 3) love of God for what God is; 4) love of self for God's sake. While at first this approach seems to focus on the individual, in actual fact it stresses the need to love self in order to be able to love others.[27]

By the sixteenth century there were many monastic groups within the Roman Catholic Church, enabling many individuals to live a simple and devoted life of monastic discipline. However, not all who had entered this monastic life had adhered strictly to the disciplines. New monastic orders, such as the Oratory of Divine Love, were established which called for greater obedience and discipline. Likewise there were calls to reform some of the existing monastic orders. For instance, St Teresa of Avila along with St John of the Cross called for a stricter observance of the Carmelite rule and founded the discalced (without shoes) Carmelites. They practised strict observance of poverty and self-denial and gave themselves to prayer. St Teresa is remembered for her writings on prayer, and her belief that followers of Jesus Christ should 'develop the habit of conscious companionship with Christ'.[28] This kind of union or communion with Christ reflects the understanding of Christian devotional writers that God is not only approachable but present.

In addition to a large number of monastic writings, there are many other types of literature such as diaries, manuals on prayer, meditations, and correspondence which offer spiritual counsel for the inward journey. All of the literature gives a clear indication that while at times an individual may need to withdraw to be alone with God, the journey of faith is also shared with others. Significantly, though, it is not shared on account of doctrinal uniformity or because all can testify to the same experience. For example, Martin Luther did not read and quote from the *Imitation of Christ* because his belief or experience was exactly like that of Thomas á Kempis. Rather what is shared between Christians, who even across the centuries know a degree of relationship in Christ, is the sense of desire or longing to know or to be known by God. While the desire to know God was at the heart of all the writings on prayer, even the manuals of prayer cannot be reduced to a simple 'how to' approach. The search for God is not simply about actively searching for and seeking God. At times there is also a need to listen in order to discern what obedience to God's call might mean.

Discerning the way of Christ

In the Bible, an emphasis on 'hearing' or discerning God's will is closely linked with the idea of obedience. For example, on one occasion Jesus told a parable of the two sons who were asked by their father to go out and work in the field. One son first said he would not go and then later changed his mind and went. The other son said yes, but did not go (Matthew 21.28–32). Those who have 'ears to hear' are those who respond to the message of Jesus. Hence, the idea in Christian faith is that God speaks and the faithful believer will 'trust and obey'. Failure to do what God requires is evidence of deafness caused by an inability to really listen and therefore discern God's way.[29]

The ability to listen so that one may discern God's voice in order to obey is a theme taken up in many Christian devotional writings. One of the most enduring examples of 'listening' and 'obeying' is found in the life of John Woolman. Born in 1720, in West Jersey in America, Woolman claimed that by the age of seven he 'began to be acquainted with the operation of divine love'.[30] Later in life he claimed he had veered toward 'youthful disobedience' but that after a period of poor health, as a young man, he had vowed that he would 'walk humbly before God'.[31] Woolman's *Journal* describes his attempt to live out a life of obedience to God. As he opened himself to listen actively to the 'Eternal Listener', he felt the only obedient response was to speak out against the many injustices within society in his day. Later he would reflect on the nature of faith which combines the inward and the outward journey, as he wrote:

> True religion consisted in an inward life, wherein the heart doth love and reverence God the Creator, and learns to exercise true justice and goodness, not only toward all men, but also toward the brute creatures; that, as the mind was moved by an inward principle to love God as an invisible, incomprehensible Being, so, by the same principle, it was moved to love him in all his manifestations in the visible world . . .[32]

Woolman was particularly disturbed by the practice of slavery especially since when he worked as a storekeeper, he was asked by his employer to write a bill of sale for a woman slave and afterwards said that he 'felt uneasy at the thoughts of writing an instrument of slavery for one of my fellow creatures'.[33] He decided that slavery was 'inconsistent with the Christian religion' and vowed that he would not engage in the activity any longer. To make others aware of the plight of slaves, he stopped wearing clothes that had been coloured with indigo dye and later stopped using rum or molasses because they were all the product of slave labour. His sensitivity to the needs of others was not limited to slaves: wherever he saw injustice, he sought to fight it. Woolman's spirituality was centred on the belief that divine love permeates the universe and that God as Holy Spirit is approachable and available to all.

Often when Woolman is discussed as an example of Quaker spirituality, he is seen as an example of individual piety and obedience. Yet times of listening to God and openness to the Spirit were never simply for his own personal benefit, but always led him out into service in the community. He travelled widely, trying to convince other Quakers of the evil of the slave trade. Moreover, his action was focused on the greater good of others within community. Religion for him was never simply an individual quest.

The Quaker tradition of coming together in silence as a group to listen provides a reminder of the wider Christian emphasis on the Spirit within the community proclaiming the word to all. In the broad Christian tradition, there is a real sense in which there is an awareness of God as the 'Eternal Listener' in our midst. There is, of course, a theological tension which arises as we open ourselves to listening in this way: it is the struggle between obedience to our understanding of the will of God and/ or the understanding of others. In other words, what happens when the Spirit of God is thought to speak in a way that is at variance with what is recognized as the will of God by other people?

Inevitably, at times, communities have tried to insist on conformity to a particular set of doctrines or a practice of worship. Yet there are moments when individuals are called by God beyond the boundaries which a community has set. But there is a very real sense in which the community often struggles to discern the mind of Christ, and to find a way to travel the road together. For some Christians, the challenge is to learn to walk together in a way that allows persons to balance individual freedom with the privilege and responsibility of fellowship with one another.

Even when Christians imagine themselves as like-minded 'pilgrim people' journeying together on the road with a particular agreed goal in mind, they are frequently at variance. Rather than walking together in perfect harmony, throughout history Christians have often found themselves striding away from those who cannot see faith in the same way.

In recognizing the possibility of conflict which occurs as communities listen and respond, it is important to note that the Church has often raised barriers which prevent such listening. This has happened historically as the Church has attempted to silence particular voices perceived as a threat to order and stability. Conformity is seen to be the easiest way to manage people. Any allowance for diversity is often perceived as a threat to authority. Real obedience, however, obedience which comes as a genuine response to what has been heard in the heart, can never be fettered.

Thomas Kelly, an American Quaker of the twentieth century, offered his readers four steps in holy obedience. The first step, he claims, is to have a 'flaming vision of the wonder of such a life'. This vision of a holy life is he claims 'the invading, urging, inviting, persuading work of the Eternal One'.[34] The second step to holy obedience he says is this: 'Begin where you are. Obey now.'[35] He argues that wherever a person may be, that person can practise 'holy obedience'. In much the same way that the monastic tradition called for ceaseless prayer, Kelly argues that a person should:

> Obey now. Use what little obedience you are capable of, even if it be like a grain of mustard seed. Begin where you are. Live this present moment, this present hour as you now sit in your seats, in utter, utter submission and openness to Him. Listen outwardly to these words, but within, behind the scenes, in the deeper levels of your lives where you are all alone with God the Loving Eternal One, keep up a silent prayer. 'Open thou my life. Guide my thoughts where I dare not let them go. But thou darest. Thy will be done.' Walk on the streets and chat with your friends. But every moment behind the scenes be in prayer, offering yourself in continuous obedience. I find this eternal continuous prayer life absolutely essential. It can be carried on day and night, in the thick of business, in home and school. Such a prayer of submission can be so simple. It is well to use a single sentence, repeated over and over and over again, such as this: 'Be thou my will. Be thou my will . . .'[36]

The third step in holy obedience is this, according to Kelly: 'If you slip and stumble and forget God for an hour, and assert your old proud self, and rely upon your own clever wisdom, don't spend too much time in anguished regrets and self-accusations but begin again, just where you are.'[37] The fourth and final step in obedience, says Kelly, is about relaxing and simply submitting to God. 'Don't grit your teeth and clench your fists and say, "I will! I will!" Relax. Take hands off. Submit yourself to God. Learn to live in the passive voice . . . for "I will" spells not obedience.'[38] This kind of obedience which Thomas Kelly calls 'holy obedience' develops out of an attentiveness to God. Kelly suggests that it begins with a profound mystical experience. Though this fades, one is left with a different vision of the world – a profound new way of seeing.

Searching for the way of Christ, as we have seen, is not simply about a momentary response to God, but rather it is a lifelong process. As a person seeks continually to respond to God, there are many turning points and twists and turns along the way which must be negotiated. This requires a willingness to listen actively in order to discern what God might be saying. It also takes patience and fortitude. The path a person should take is not always obvious, in spite of the fact that he or she may have been listening and seeking to be obedient to God. Baron Friedrich Von Hügel offered three images which helped him in what he called the 'flinty furlong'.[39] At 18 years of age, he claimed that he discovered that the way of faith was rather like climbing a mountain. An experienced mountain climber will take short, even steps and when the fog and thick mists come and it is impossible to see where to go, the climber stops and waits until the fog lifts. In his 30s, Von Hügel said he discovered another image which helped him enormously. It was the image of being on board a ship in a small cabin with a few selected items that could be tied down during the storm and provide stability. The last image, Von Hügel said, came to him in his 40s. He said that he imagined travelling across the desert on a camel. When a sand storm comes, the experienced traveller does not try to battle the storm, but gets off the camel and lies prostrate on the sand with head covered until the storm passes. Whatever happens he said:

> whether it be great cloud-mists on the mountain side, or huge, mountain-high waves on the ocean, or blinding sand storms in the desert; there is each time one crucial point – to form no conclusions, to take no decisions, to change nothing during such crises, and, especially at such times, not to force any particularly religious mood or idea in oneself. To turn gently to other things, to maintain a vague, general attitude of resignation – to be very meek, with oneself and with others: the crisis goes by, thus, with great fruit. What is a religion worth which costs you nothing? What is a sense of God worth which would be at your disposal, capable of being comfortably elicited when and where you please? It is far, far more God who must hold us, than we who hold him.[40]

Von Hügel knew that suffering and hardship was part of the Christian way. Yet he was sure that God would remain steadfast in every circumstance. To this theme we will turn in the next chapter.

Draw your own conclusions

What do you think Christians mean by being 'in the world' and 'not of the world'?

Reflect on the idea of pilgrimage or journey in Christian spirituality. How might the inward journey and the outward journey be combined?

Simplicity of life and asceticism were important features of the spirituality of the Desert Mothers and Fathers. Do you think these are still meaningful to Christian spirituality today?

Look again at George Herbert's 'love poem' which Simone Weil said became her prayer. How is God portrayed in the poem? What kind of relationship is depicted in the poem?

Reflect on the link between 'hearing' and 'obedience' in Christian spirituality. How could John Woolman's desire for social justice be a reflection of his obedience to a 'call'?

Further reading

Writings about the Desert Fathers and Mothers and monasticism

Louis Bouyer (1960), *The Spirituality of the New Testament and the Fathers*, A History of Christian Spirituality, Vol. 1, London: Burns & Oates.

Douglas Burton-Christie (1993), *The Word in the Desert: Scripture and the Quest for Holiness in Early Christian Monasticism*, Oxford: Oxford University Press.

Derwas J. Chitty (1968), *The Desert A City: An Introduction to the Study of Egyptian and Palestinian Monasticism under the Christian Empire*, Oxford: Oxford University Press.

Marilyn Dunn (2000), *The Emergence of Monasticism: From the Desert Fathers to the Early Middle Ages*, Oxford: Blackwell.

Thomas Merton (1960), *The Wisdom of the Desert: Sayings from the Desert Fathers of the Fourth Century*, New York: New Directions Books.

Benedicta Ward tr. (1975), *The Desert Christian: Sayings of the Desert Fathers*, New York: Macmillan.

Benedicta Ward (1986), *The Wisdom of the Desert Fathers*, Oxford, SLG Press.

Rowan Williams (2003), *Silence and Honey Cakes: The Wisdom of the Desert*, Oxford: Lion Publishing.

Vincent Wimbush and Richard Valantasis (eds) (1995), *Asceticism*, Oxford: Oxford University Press.

Celtic spirituality

Oliver Davies (1999), *Celtic Spirituality*, Classics of Western Spirituality, New York: Paulist Press.

Ian Bradley (1999), *Celtic Christianity: Making Myths and Chasing Dreams*, Edinburgh: Edinburgh University Press.

Esther De Waal (1991), *A World Made Whole: Discovering the Celtic Tradition*, London: HarperCollins.

Brendan O'Malley (2002), *A Celtic Primer: The Complete Celtic Worship Resource and Collection*, Norwich: Canterbury Press.

Spiritual direction

Peter Ball (1996), *Journey into Truth, Spiritual Direction in the Anglican Tradition*, London: Mowbray Press.

David G. Benner (2002), *Sacred Companions, The Gift of Spiritual Friendship and Direction*, Downers Grove: Intervarsity Press.

Mary Dougherty, SSND (1995), *Group Spiritual Direction*, Mahwah, New Jersey: Paulist Press.

Tilden Edwards (1980), *Spiritual Friend*, New York: Paulist Press.

Tilden Edwards (2001), *Spiritual Director: Spiritual Companion,* Mahwah, New Jersey: Paulist Press.

Margaret Guenther (1992), *Holy Listening: The Art of Spiritual Direction*, Cambridge, Mass.: Cowley Publications.

Morton Kelsey (1983), *Companions on the Inner Way: The Art of Spiritual Direction*, New York: Crossroad.

Kenneth Leech (1977), *Soul Friend: A Study of Spirituality*, London: Sheldon Press.

Eugene Peterson (1989), *The Contemplative Pastor: Returning to the Art of Spiritual Direction*, Dallas: Word.

Janet Ruffing (2000), *Spiritual Direction: Beyond the Beginnings*, Mahwah, New Jersey: Paulist Press.

Worship

Christopher Cocksworth (1997), *Holy, Holy, Holy: Worshipping the Trinitarian God*, London: Darton, Longman & Todd.

Christopher Ellis (2004), *Gathering: A Theology and Spirituality of Worship in the Free Church Tradition*, London: SCM Press.

Cheslyn Jones, Geoffrey Wainwright and Edward Yarnold, SJ (1978), *The Study of Liturgy*, Oxford: Oxford University Press.

Gordon Wakefield (1998), *An Outline of Christian Worship*, Edinburgh: T&T Clark.

James White (1980/1990), *Introduction to Christian Worship*, revd edn, Nashville: Abingdon Press.

Notes

1 John Dunne (1987), *The Homing Spirit: A Pilgrimage of the Mind, of the Heart, of the Soul*, New York: Crossroad, p. 55.

2 Marjorie J. Thompson (1995), *Soul Feast*, Louisville: Westminster/John Knox, p. 47.

3 John Bunyan, *The Pilgrim's Progress*, ed. with an introduction by Roger Sharrock (1965 reprinted 1981), Aylesbury: Penguin Books, pp. 98–9.

4 Gordon Mursell (2001), *English Spirituality: From Earliest Times to 1700*, London: SPCK, p. 411.

5 See Romans 5.10–11; 1 Corinthians 1.18; 6.11; Romans 8.23–24; 2 Corinthians 1.22; Ephesians 1.13–14; Philippians 1.6.

6 Dag Hammarskjöld (1964), *Markings*, New York: Ballantine Books, p. 180.

7 To give one example, the idea of a morphology of conversion was suggested in the seventeenth century by the Puritan preacher William Perkins. Michael J. Watts (1978), *The Dissenters: Volume I, From the Reformation to the French Revolution*, Oxford: Clarendon Press, p. 174, says 'the process of conversion

expounded by Perkins was upheld by English Evangelicals for three centuries as normative of Christian experience'. The Puritan conversion narrative has also been explored in Charles Loyd Cohen (1986), *God's Caress: the Psychology of the Puritan Religious Experience*, Oxford: Oxford University Press, and Patricia Caldwell (1983), *The Puritan Conversion Narrative, the Beginnings of the American Expression*, Cambridge: Cambridge University Press.

8 Simone Weil (1951), *Waiting On God*, Glasgow: HarperCollins, pp. 25, 27.

9 George Herbert, *The Country Parson, The Temple*, ed. John N. Wall, Jr (1981), New York: Paulist Press, p. 316.

10 Weil, *Waiting On God*, p. 25.

11 Weil, *Waiting On God*, pp. 66–7.

12 Blaise Pascal (1966), 'The Memorial', in *Pensées*, tr. with introduction A. J. Krailsheimer, Harmondsworth: Penguin Books, pp. 309–10.

13 Pascal, *Pensées*, p. 85.

14 Pascal, *Pensées*, p. 85.

15 Pascal, *Pensées*, p. 85.

16 John Henry Newman, *Apologia Pro Vita Sua: Being a History of His Religious Opinions*, ed. Martin J. Svaglic (1967), Oxford: Clarendon Press, pp. 90–214 as cited in Hugh T. Kerr and John M. Mulder (1983), *Conversions*, Grand Rapids: William Eerdmans, p. 128.

17 J. H. Newman, 'Lead, kindly light', in *The Baptist Hymn Book* (1962), London: Psalms and Hymns Trust.

18 Joseph A. Jungmann (1978), *Christian Prayer through the Centuries*, New York: Paulist Press, pp. 7–8.

19 Jungmann, *Christian Prayer*, p. 1.

20 Laura Swan (2001), *The Forgotten Desert Mothers*, Mahwah, New Jersey: Paulist Press, p. 21.

21 Swan, *Desert Mothers*, p. 26.

22 Yushi Nomura (1983), *Desert Wisdom, Sayings from Desert Fathers*, London: Eyre and Spottiswoode, p. 45.

23 Athanasius, 'Life of Antony', in Philip Schaff and Henry Wace (eds) (1991), *A Select Library of Nicene and Post-Nicene Fathers of The Christian Church*, Edinburgh, T&T Clark, p. 199.

24 Ian Bradley (2000), *Colonies of Heaven*, London: Darton, Longman & Todd, p. 233.

25 Jungmann, *Christian Prayer*, p. 21.

26 John Cassian, 'The first Conference of Abbot Isaac', chapter 3 in Schaff and Wace (eds), *Nicene and Post-Nicene Fathers*, p. 388.

27 Bernard of Clairvaux, 'On the Love of God', in Ray C. Petry (ed.) (1962), *Late Medieval Mysticism*, Library of Christian Classics, London: SCM Press, pp. 60–6.

28 Rowan Williams (1991), *Teresa of Avila*, London: Geoffrey Chapman, p. 91.

29 See Psalm 115.6; Isaiah 6.9–10; Matthew 11.15; Mark 4.9; Luke 14.35.

30 John Woolman (1774), *The Journal of John Woolman*, The John Greenleaf Whitter edition (1961), introduction by Fredrick B. Tolles, Secaucus, New Jersey: The Citadel Press, p. v.

31 Woolman, *Journal*, p. 8.

32 Woolman, *Journal*, p. 14.

33 Woolman, *Journal*, p. 14.

34 Thomas Kelly (1941), *A Testament of Devotion*, New York: Harper and Brothers, p. 59.

35 Kelly, *Testament*, p. 60.

36 Kelly, *Testament*, p. 60.

37 Kelly, *Testament*, p. 61.

38 Kelly, *Testament*, p. 61.

39 Friedrich Von Hügel (1945/1964), *Selected Writings*, London: Collins Fontana, p. 84.

40 Von Hügel, *Selected Writings*, pp. 84–5.

5

The Suffering of Christ and Our Suffering

I have a friend who lost her husband quite suddenly while they were on holiday. It was a terrible shock and in the days and months that followed she struggled to come to terms with her grief. One day she told me that the death of her husband had caused her to think about faith in God. She had gone to church since childhood and had always believed there was a God, but now she was not so sure. 'If there is a God', she said, 'why did God allow this to happen and where is God now?' Many people have experiences that cause them to think again about belief in God.

Sometimes questions like these seem to strike at the very heart of Christian faith, especially if people think that religious belief will ensure a trouble-free life. There are people who accept Christian belief on the understanding that if a person repents, receives forgiveness, and trusts in God, then life will be happy, free from sorrow or suffering and devoid of pain. This type of thought, though sometimes popularly promoted, not only denies the reality of human existence, but it is completely at odds with biblical teaching. Far from escaping suffering, human beings are born into the midst of tears of joy and pain and it seems that throughout life both delight and sorrow may be experienced.

Christians not only face suffering, but they also grapple with the theological issues that emerge when confronted with the problem of suffering: if God is a God of love, why do people suffer? Where is God in suffering? Does God cause the suffering? How are we to understand human suffering in Christian spirituality? These are difficult questions which have led theologians to spend many hours struggling with the nature of God.

John V. Taylor told of one occasion when he was asked by a friend to visit a young couple whose two-year-old daughter had been found dead in her cot. Taylor says that as they asked the questions 'why?' and 'why her?', he could not claim to them that it was all part of God's providence and that one day they would understand. Rather, he said to them that:

> their child's death was a tragic accident, an unforeseeable failure in the functioning of the little body; that so far from being willed or planned by God, it was for him a disaster and a frustration of his will for life and fulfillment, just as it was for them, that God shared their pain and

loss and was with them in it. I went on to say that God is not a poten-
tate ordering this or that to happen, but that the world is full of chance
and accident and God has let it be so because that is the only sort of
world in which freedom, development, responsibility and love could
come into being, but that God was committed to this kind of world
in love and to each person in it, and was with them in their tragedy,
giving himself to them in fortitude and healing and faith to help them
through. And their child was held in that same caring, suffering love.[1]

While today many Christians draw great comfort from the belief that
when individuals suffer they are not alone, rather God suffers with them,
this has not always been the case. In the past, some Christians found it difficult to believe that God could be affected by, and subject to, the suffering
of the world. Yet the horrors of the World Wars, genocide and suffering on
an unprecedented global scale in the twentieth century caused people to
consider that God might be vulnerable and open to the pain and suffering
of all creation. God, as Jürgen Moltmann put it, is the 'crucified God'.[2]

It is difficult for some people to accept that God suffers. Yet, as John
Macquarrie has pointed out, perhaps what we might consider to be 'the
"weakness of God", the God who manifests himself in the crucified Christ'
by 'placing himself at the mercy of the world' is actually the strength of
God.[3] Not only is God a God of love, who risks all and gives all for the
sake of love, but we are called to the same self-giving way. More than
simply recognizing that God is with us in our suffering, Rowan Williams
has suggested that 'This is the great challenge to faith: knowing that
Christ is in the heart of darkness, we are called to go there with him.'[4]

The idea of a 'suffering God' can only be understood, of course, in the
context of relationship, and in particular the relationship of God which
we call Trinity. The purpose of this chapter, however, is not to explore the
nature of God, to examine theodicy, or to try to establish a theological
justification for suffering.[5] Rather, building on the affirmation that God
is at the heart of suffering, this chapter will explore some of the issues for
Christian spirituality which emerge when one accepts that suffering is
part of living within a community of faith.

Suffering as choice?

Suffering is part of the human condition. Sometimes human beings are
responsible for the suffering they and others experience. On other occasions, they are simply the victims of circumstance. Sometimes, however,

suffering is by choice. In a thought-provoking article, entitled 'When Prayer Encounters Pain', Flora Slosson Wuellner suggested that there are at least five major categories of human suffering which she labelled as: 'the thorn in the flesh', 'the hunger', 'the catapult', 'the cross' and 'the birth'.[6] The first three types of suffering, as the names suggest, are types of suffering that she claims may be faced as part of being human. 'The thorn in the flesh', for instance, refers to the kind of suffering caused by illness. Likewise, 'the hunger' depicts a type of suffering that may rise out of some sort of emotional or physical deprivation, such as a broken relationship or as Wuellner puts it: the 'pain of those who have not loved enough or for whom love has meant constriction rather than freedom'.[7] 'The catapult' is a symbol of suffering caused by a traumatic encounter with evil and injustice.

Wuellner's final two types of suffering are distinguished from the earlier three in that they are not simply suffering as part of the human condition, but rather suffering which is embraced when one specifically chooses to follow the Christian way. These are: 'the cross' and 'the birth'. 'The cross', according to Wuellner, is suffering that is experienced when one consciously chooses to enter into the pain of another person. 'The birth' is suffering caused by the 'awakening, stretching or rebirth of our deepest inner selves'.[8] She says it is 'the pain of endings and beginnings', it is the pain of 'letting go and taking hold'.[9]

To attach a label to a type of suffering, as Wuellner has done, is not to trivialize or underestimate the misery and anguish that people experience. Nor is it to suggest that simply by naming it, we have explained what the suffering must be like. It is impossible to find adequate words to express the depth of human distress. Yet in trying to understand how suffering is part of Christian spirituality, it is helpful to make a distinction between suffering that is part of the human condition and suffering that comes as part of the choice to follow the Christian way. Wuellner claims that 'the cross' and 'the birth' are types of suffering that God 'invites us to', rather than suffering that occurs without our choice.[10] Suffering which God invites us to? Yes, this is suffering that is embraced as a necessary part of the Christian pilgrimage and through it a person may find joy.

Suffering as part of the Christian journey

The theme of suffering which is part of 'the birth' is closely linked to the New Testament idea of finding 'new life in Christ'. The Gospel writers give accounts of the women who went to the tomb where the body of

Jesus had been placed and found it empty. There they met the risen Christ and they are portrayed as awakening to new life out of the darkness of grief and despair. The Apostle Paul would later describe the experience of being buried with Christ in baptism and rising to walk in newness of life (Romans 6.4). This new birth is described in different ways by Christians. Some people speak of the choice to follow the suffering Christ as 'another chance', or a 'new beginning', or a 'fresh start'. However a person may describe it, the idea of rebirth or being 'born again' represents a new life which may be discovered by those who have experienced sorrow and suffering. This is what John Newton (1725–1807), the ex-slave trader who became a Christian minister, was trying to convey when he wrote:

How sweet the Name of Jesus sounds
    in a believer's ear!
It soothes his sorrows, heals his wounds,
    and drives away his fear.

It makes the wounded spirit whole,
    and calms the troubled breast;
'tis manna to the hungry soul,
    and to the weary, rest.

Dear Name, the rock on which I build,
    my shield and hiding-place,
my never-failing treasury, filled
    with boundless stores of grace!

Jesus! my Shepherd, Brother, Friend,
    my Prophet, Priest and King,
my Lord, my Life, my Way, my End,
    accept the praise I bring.

Weak is the effort of my heart,
    and cold my warmest thought;
but when I see thee as thou art,
    I'll praise thee as I ought.

Till then I would thy love proclaim
    with every fleeting breath;
and may the music of thy Name
    refresh my soul in death![11]

In addition to choosing suffering which may result in seeing life in a new way or feeling as if one has been offered a new beginning, there is also the suffering of the cross. Gordon Mursell has pointed out that in late medieval spirituality (1300–1500) the inner or 'interior journey' of Christian discipleship and devotion was often a journey within the suffering of Christ.[12] This was a journey to be made by the individual who was willing to turn from any desire for riches and wealth and seek to meditate on the wounds and passion of Christ and thereby in some way to identify with the sufferings of Christ. To do this meant that a person not only realized the depth of God's love for humanity which was demonstrated in the suffering of Christ, but also, by meditating on the suffering of Christ, that one was drawn into a closer relationship with him.

Focusing on the suffering of Christ and identifying with it to the point of entering into it, confirmed the belief that while suffering was part of the journey of life, nothing could separate believers from the love of God in Christ. This idea of meditating on the wounds of Christ and being drawn into them as a way of receiving comfort and solace developed, of course, in a period when there was a great deal of suffering caused by the 'Black Death' (the name given to the plague which swept across Europe in the mid-fourteenth century, killing a large number of the population). The fear and insecurity brought about by the plague, as Mursell points out, was compounded by social and political unrest resulting in peasant uprisings and the Hundred Years War.[13]

By focusing on suffering as part of the interior life, one was able to accept and even find meaning in the actual physical suffering that might come. Moreover, the discipline of identifying with Christ in experiences of suffering as part of both the inner and the outer world were a way of deepening faith and drawing nearer to God. As one dwelt on suffering in the inner world, when actual physical suffering came, it was seen as something that could lead one to a new understanding of God's way and purposes. It is not always clear from the medieval devotional writings if such suffering is supposed to be seen as an accident or something God ordained or just allowed. However, the point is that any suffering could be a means through which a person drew nearer to God.

An example of suffering that was used by God can be seen, for instance, in the writing of Mother Julian of Norwich, the fourteenth-century mystic who, at the age of 30, experienced a physical illness which gripped her for three days and nights. She was so ill that it appeared she would die and it was then that she had a series of visions on which she would meditate for 20 years. Published as *Revelations of Divine Love*, her meditations speak of 'deeds which are committed which in our eyes are so evil and lead to so much harm that it seems impossible that any good could come out of them'.[14] Yet Mother Julian says Christ revealed to her that he would 'make all things well'.[15] She admits that she could not see how it could happen, but the answer God gave to her in this revelation was that:

> 'What is impossible to you is not impossible to me. I will keep my word, in every detail, and I shall make all things well.' So God taught me by grace that I should stand fast in faith as I had understood it before, and believe firmly that all things will be well, as our Lord had revealed to me.[16]

Through the centuries, Christians have had different ways of understanding the place of suffering in human experience. At times, Christians have seen illness to be a punishment for sin. They believed that when they were ill or when some tragedy struck, God was meting out punishment for some past failure. This understanding of God does not sit well with a picture of a God of love and many Christians would not equate illness or misfortune with punishment, nor would they claim tragedy was in any way caused by an act of God's will. Nevertheless, the suffering in itself might be embraced and through it one might discover anew the love of a God who weeps with us and at the same time is always seeking to 'make all things well'.

Often when we think of suffering, particularly as we reflect on the experience of someone like Mother Julian, it is tempting to think of suffering as a personal experience. It is something that is particular to an individual and specific to a context and time. There are few things less helpful in a conversation over some grief or loss than for someone to say 'I know how you feel'. On one occasion I went to see the family of a young woman who had died from cancer. While the young woman had a deep commitment to Jesus Christ, the other members of the family did not openly confess Christian faith. As I sat with the family, in anger the young woman's brother said to me, 'well can you say anything?' I looked at him, 'No', I said, 'I can't'. I suppose there are some who would argue that it was a moment for speaking about the love of God which reaches even into the darkness of pain and sorrow. Or perhaps it was a time to say that the Bible tells us that nothing 'will be able to separate us from the love of God in Christ Jesus our Lord' (Romans 8.39). Later I would say those things, but at that moment, it seemed right simply to sit in the silence. This is the silence of the cross.

To suggest that one loss is similar to another, or can in any sense be understood, is to deny the uniqueness of human relationship. Suffering, of course, is personal and particular, but in terms of Christian faith it is never private, for all suffering is in some sense gathered up and meets in the suffering of Christ.

Bound together in the suffering of Christ

The New Testament witness emphasizes that Christian believers were drawn together in and through the death and resurrection of Christ. That means that the Church is not simply people who have come together in order to pray and worship. Rather, at a fundamental level they are united in Christ. As we have already seen, the idea of union 'in Christ' means that believers have a deep relatedness to others because of the death and resurrection of Christ. Among many Christians, it has sometimes been overlooked that this unity of believers in Christ is also linked to shared suffering.

In the Western Christian Church today, perhaps especially among the affluent and prosperous communities of faith, it appears that very little is said about unity in and through the suffering of Christ. People speak of being drawn to a particular congregation because of the form of worship or the style of preaching or activities offered there, but rarely is mention made of being gathered by God into community, let alone of being united in suffering. It may be, of course, that for some people suffering is something which has been looked upon as deeply personal. It is so personal, in fact, that it may be argued that suffering often seems to separate us from others. However, the biblical witness and the witness of many Christians is that shared suffering within the body of Christ not only deepens our relationship to Christ, but through Christ we are united to one another. We are to share in the sufferings of one another. This came home to me in a startling way on one occasion when I sat in the Sheldonian Theatre in Oxford and heard John V. Taylor relate a story about Sister Frances Dominica. She works at Helen House, a hospice for children in Oxford, and he described the experience she had related to him in her own words:

I had known this mother for some time as both her daughters suffered from a rare genetic illness, and were frequent visitors to Helen House. During the year she and her husband went through a difficult and painful divorce. On Christmas morning she telephoned and I went. Her 13-year-old died the following morning, suddenly and unexpectedly. Seeing her sister dead, the four-year-old said, 'I wanted to die first', and five days later she too died. During those days and nights that I was with the mother and her children there were a thousand and one things to do. After the funeral there was nothing to do except to be there beside her. Surrounded by grief too immense for words, I felt physical pain which still recurs from time to time when I least expect it. By staying alongside I was absorbing a little of her pain.[17]

It seems to me that this story points to something of the real sharing 'in Christ'. Taylor claims that by 'surrendering himself to death he [Jesus Christ] drew it into himself and absorbed it'. So if, in Christ, we come alongside others in their suffering, we may find that 'pain or despair is drawn off from one to another, while endurance and hope flows from the other to the one'.[18]

The cross for Christians has become a symbol of selfless, suffering love. It serves as a reminder that the love which journeyed with the people of Israel, the love which spoke through the prophets, is a love that continues to reach out to human beings across the span of time. Mother Julian expressed this act of love so beautifully when she wrote:

Then our good Lord Jesus Christ asked, 'Are you pleased because I suffered for you?' I said, 'Yes, I am, Lord, thank you. Yes, dear Lord, I praise you.' And then our Lord Jesus, our kind Lord, said, 'If you are glad, then so am I. It gives me great joy and happiness, it is perpetual delight to have suffered for you. If I could suffer more I would.' . . . In his words, 'If I could suffer more, I would', I saw that if need be he would have died over and over again, and his love would have given him no rest till he had done so. And I looked hard to see how many times he would have died. But the number was so way beyond my comprehension that I could not take it in. Yet no matter how many times he had died he would have dismissed it as nothing because of his love of us. Compared to his great love all else seems infinitesimal . . . For the suffering was a noble, glorious act of love, worked out in time, but love itself is outside time, it was without beginning and will have no conclusion. It was because of this love that he said so sweetly, 'If I could suffer more, I would have.' He did not say, 'If it were necessary to suffer more', for even if it were not necessary, he would have suffered more, if he could have. This act and this work for our salvation was arranged as well as God could arrange it. For in Christ I saw complete joy and his joy would not have been complete if it could have been done in any better way.[19]

It is a paradox of the Christian faith that love and suffering are inextricably linked. Only as individuals embrace the suffering that comes as followers of Christ will they know the joy of life in him. Love and joy are discovered in the midst of pain and hardship. Perhaps this is, in part, what Dietrich Bonhoeffer meant when he wrote that 'the cross is not the terrible end to an otherwise God-fearing and happy life, but it meets us at the beginning of our communion with Christ'. When Christ calls a person, 'he bids them come and die'.[20] He also claimed:

> To endure the cross is not a tragedy; it is suffering which is the fruit of exclusive allegiance to Jesus Christ. When it comes, it is not an accident, but a necessity. It is not the sort of suffering, which is inseparable from this mortal life, but the suffering which is an essential part of the specifically Christian life . . . Discipleship means allegiance to the suffering Christ, and it is therefore not at all surprising that Christians should be called upon to suffer. In fact it is a joy and a token of his grace.[21]

Bonhoeffer stresses that the believer will not necessarily understand all that might be faced as a follower of Christ. In his view, a person is not supposed to understand everything:

> Discipleship is not limited to what you can comprehend – it must transcend all comprehension. Plunge into the deep waters beyond your own comprehension, and I will help you to comprehend even as I do. Bewilderment is true comprehension. Not to know where you are going is true knowledge.[22]

The call to follow Christ is, of course, an individual choice, but as we have already seen, it is not a solitary pilgrimage. The call to follow is the call to be in community with others who also follow. And the community, if it is indeed a community of and with and in Christ, will be a community acquainted with suffering.

The cross and the new community: the New Testament witness

From its beginning, a central tenet of the Christian faith has been that believers are brought together as one body in the death and resurrection of Christ. Yet it seems that while Christians have always affirmed the centrality of the cross and resurrection, they have struggled to understand the meaning of the suffering of Jesus. Indeed the cross appeared to be scandalous to many early Christians. At times it seems that they were ready to cast aside the message of the cross as foolishness (1 Corinthians

1.18). For instance, the Apostle Paul seemed to believe that the reason for the divisions within the Church in Corinth could be traced back to their failure to comprehend the meaning of a crucified Christ. Hence, he wrote to them urging them to keep the cross at the centre of their life together.

In her commentary on the Gospel according to Mark, Morna Hooker suggests that it may well have been the temptation to glory in the Christian life and to neglect the suffering of the cross within the Markan community which led the Gospel writer to give so much attention to the passion of Christ.[23] Over and over in that Gospel account, we find Jesus telling his disciples that he must undergo great suffering and be killed and after three days rise again. Each time the disciples seem unable to understand. They continue to seek human power and recognition, even when they are called upon to take up the cross and follow (Mark 8.31–38; 9.30–37). The disciples, it seems, found the message of the weakness of the cross and a suffering Saviour too much to bear.

For Christians, the death of Christ on the cross and his resurrection on the third day is the way God has demonstrated his love for all people. The continuing presence of God's Spirit in the lives of people today is a sign of God's ongoing love and desire to reconcile all things to himself. The idea of reconciliation with God by means of the life, death and resurrection of Christ has been interpreted by Christians in different ways. Some people think primarily of the atoning work of the cross in terms of sacrifice, while others speak in terms of the work of Christ as vicarious, that is that it was in place of the sinner. Still others reflect on the atoning work of Christ as being representative. While our purpose here is not to discuss all the doctrinal arguments for theories of atonement, it is worth noting that often the language that has been used to discuss the cross has been individualistic. While the message of Christian faith is certainly personal and calls for an individual response in repentance and faith, the work of the cross is never to be understood primarily in individualistic terms.

The New Testament witnesses bear testimony to the fact that the one outcome of the suffering of Christ was the formation of a new community; the formation of a new covenant people. The concept of a new covenant community is central to understanding God's enduring suffering love. Like the covenant of God with the people of old, Christians believe that the promise is made for all God's people. Personal commitment and faith is necessary, but equally important is the idea that God's people have been joined together in the suffering love of God. God has drawn a people together as God has always done through enduring steadfast love. Christians believe that the love that journeyed with the people of Israel, the love that agonized through the witness of the prophets over the lack of faithfulness of the people, is the same love that reached out to the hurting and troubled world and then walked the road to Gethsemane and Golgotha. It is a love that seeks to draw all people to it, even as they turn to flee. It is a love that suffers and through suffering continues to draw people together into one.

'Bearing one another's burdens': life in a covenant community

Christian faith teaches that people are united to Christ not simply by personal experience and confession of faith (for most Christians through baptism), but also corporately; since in fellowship, believers are a part of the whole body of Christ, the Church. While Christians have identified and expressed the visible body of Christ in different ways, many would argue that relationship in and through Christ with others finds its deepest expression when people recognize that because of Christ, they are connected to others. This is not a superficial sense of being connected because others call themselves Christian, rather, this is a relatedness to others who bear the image of God and indeed with the whole created order that holds together in Christ. Hence, in this relationship in Christ, an individual would not speak of attending a local church, but of being called by Christ into a community of faith.

Those who take this approach have argued that one can only speak of Church as community to which one has been called. It is a community of believers drawn together by God to seek the way of Christ together. This emphasis on 'the congregational way' stresses that the Church is a society or fellowship of believers who profess a willingness to give themselves in relationship to the Lord and to one another and allowed Scripture to be their guide for faith and practice. Baptists drew up covenant agreements among the believers in local churches which professed their belief that they had been called together to share life in Christ and which spoke of a real sharing in the suffering of others. For example, in her diary, an eighteenth-century Baptist woman claimed that as she reflected on her experience of sharing in the Lord's Supper she felt that

> . . . the concerns of others goes very near my soul such as I hope have an interest in Christ. When I know their temptations, their afflictions or their consolations, I seem to bear an equal share in either, and how can it be otherwise when I look upon them together with myself as part of the purchase of Christ's suffering and so a part of that real body of whom Christ is the head.[24]

However one understands ecclesiology, Christians understand that for a community of faith to share in the burdens of Christ, there must be a real sharing (a communion) in and through Christ and with other people. This kind of sharing in Christ should call people beyond denominational boundaries or doctrinal differences. While fellowship in Christ has been depicted primarily as sharing in worship and particularly through table fellowship, these may simply be outward expressions of a deeper union in Christ through suffering.

For the early Church, fellowship (*koinonia*) in Christ through sharing in suffering was clearly part of their life together. Indeed, this is what compassion means: to share in the sufferings of another. So the Apostle Paul, writing to the Christians in Philippi, spoke of the way they shared with him in the gospel and told them that God had graciously granted them the privilege not only of believing in Christ, but of suffering for him as well (Philippians 1.29). To the Christians in Corinth, he wrote that they shared in his suffering, that is in his 'afflictions as well as his consolations' (2 Corinthians 1.3–7). In Acts, we read that the Apostles were flogged and ordered not to speak in the name of Jesus and when they left, they 'rejoiced that they were considered worthy to suffer dishonour for the sake of the name' of Christ (Acts 5.41).

The idea of sharing in the suffering of Christ was taken still further by some of the early Christian writers, particularly when Christians faced persecution for their beliefs. Tertullian, writing in the early third century, claimed that the blood of the martyrs might indeed be seen as baptism in blood for those who had not been baptized in water. Origen, in writing of martyrdom, seemed to imply that the death of the martyr could be likened to the death of Christ for the world. He wrote: 'Baptism in the form of martyrdom, as received by the saviour, is a purgation for the world; so too, when we receive it, it becomes a purgation for many.'[25] Martyrdom came to be seen as an expression of sharing with Christ in suffering. Moreover, for many, it came to be seen as the highest form of Christian service.

While the theme of suffering in and through Christ is at the heart of Christian spirituality, as we have already seen in the example of Sister Frances Dominica cited earlier, we may not speak lightly of the idea of 'shared suffering' or leave the impression that suffering may easily be embraced or that it is possible to simply enter into the sufferings of others. While it is true that in some sense suffering may unite believers to one another, it is also true that there is a very real sense in which suffering separates us from others simply because we cannot completely enter into the suffering of others. This sense of isolation in suffering is described by Nicholas Wolterstorff as he reflects on the death of his son, Eric, in a mountaineering accident:

> I have been daily grateful for the friend who remarked that grief iso-lates. He did not mean only that I, grieving, am isolated from you, happy. He meant also that 'shared' grief isolates the sharers from each other. Though united in that we are grieving, we grieve differently. As each death has its own character, so too each grief over a death has its own character – its own inscape . . .[26]

There is a sense in which Wolterstorff is right. Grief separates. How can we share in the anguish of a friend who has lost his spouse? How can we enter into the pain of someone who is suffering daily in her battle with terminal illness? How can those who always lived amidst wealth and affluence feel the pain and sorrow of those who watch their children die of malnutrition? There is a very real sense in which suffering separates us from one another.

For Christians, part of the mystery of the passion of Christ and the suffering experienced on the cross is that here God experienced both the separation and embrace of love. And now, God is with us even in moments when we feel cut off from others and from God. For Christians, this is partly expressed in the witness of the New Testament as we trace the steps of Jesus through the loneliness of a place called Gethsemane where he went to pray, to the moment when his friends all turned and fled, to the hour when he hung on the cross and cried out, 'My God, My God, why have you forsaken me?' (Mark 15.34). The New Testament does not hide the suffering and separation of the cross. In fact as Eduard Schweizer has commented, in Mark's Gospel, 'following' as the disciples are called to do in some sense means a participation in Jesus' vocation of suffering and death (Mark 10.32).[27]

Yet the final word in Christian faith is not death, but life. Even as we hear the strange cry from the cross which seems to separate God from God, Christian faith asserts that the cry of isolation is also the cry that draws us together into one. Christians believe that there is a unity of God with humankind in covenant love which cannot be broken. As Teilhard de Chardin put it: 'Christ binds us and reveals us to one another.'[28] It is this profound togetherness in the suffering of Christ which deeply unites Christians. This is certainly what Christianity claims – we are deeply bound to one another not because of our ability to keep certain rules or find agreement on every point of doctrine or ethics or because we ap-proach worship in the same way, but because of the suffering of Christ.

In this chapter, we have considered that the way of being Christian is the way of being bound to others through the unity of shared life in Christ. This means that one participates with others within community having been drawn together through the death and resurrection of Christ. The idea of sharing together in suffering is one which may be especially important to a community of faith. Perhaps rightly so, for it is within the bounds of day-to-day living that one is brought close to the pain and sorrow of others. Yet it may be argued that this has wider implications for the way a Christian approaches the whole of life.

Sharing in the suffering community

Sometimes, when exploring the spirituality of earlier generations, there is a temptation to portray their experience in a favourable light and to imply that it represents some ideal to which the modern Church should now aspire. Great care should be taken because, as we have already seen, the story of others is not necessarily to be emulated and the past should not be viewed through rose-tinted glasses. There are many examples of those who have claimed to be Christian believers who have not shared with others in suffering, or who, indeed, at times have brought great suffering on others.

There are many reasons why the idea of sharing in the suffering of Christ has been neglected. Sometimes it is because faith is viewed as purely individual and private and something that does not require engagement with others. Sometimes there is no real sharing in the body of Christ because they understand the Church as an institutional entity (e.g. the place I go to worship, the doctrines to which I aspire, the denomination to which I belong) rather than as being part of the living body of Christ. Sometimes as a result of the emphasis on church leaders as the primary (and often paid and therefore 'professional') support workers and hence the ones who are assigned the task of bearing the burdens of others, church members assume little, if any, real responsibility. There are deeper issues, too, which are usually related to differences in scriptural interpretation or doctrine. For instance, some people have theological differences in the way they understand the sacraments, particularly baptism and the Lord's Supper. Since there is a very broad range of views on the nature and even the necessity of the sacraments, at times they have been used as a way of excluding others rather than drawing people together in shared suffering. For instance, some Christians such as members of the Society of Friends do not practise baptism or the Lord's Supper. George Fox (1624–91), the founder of the Quakers, emphasized the need to be open to God as Holy Spirit and called for religion to be freed from the 'steeple houses'! Later Quakers argued that all of life might be seen as a sacrament.[29]

The existence of the Quakers, as well as other non-sacramental groups like the Salvation Army, serve as a reminder that however important baptism and the Lord's Supper might be to some Christians, it is not the outward participation in rite or ritual that reflects participation in Christ. Conformity or non-conformity to doctrinal belief or tradition should not necessarily militate against a real sharing in the body of Christ. The real issue is seeing participation in a community of faith as an expression of a participation in God as well as an incorporation into the body of Christ. That is to say, it is to know that what binds people together is the belief in and experience of (in all its richness and variety) a living Christ.

This concept of being bound in and through Christ to others and to all creation is far easier to speak about than to put into practice. In fact, there are many instances when an individual might feel that it is quite impossible to bear the burdens of another. For instance, if one does not agree with the particular interpretation of Scripture which has led to the suffering of another, is a Christian still bound to enter into the other person's suffering? Can a person be separated from the suffering of another if one believes the cause of suffering is based on a misuse of freedom? An example of what I mean, may be taken from the nineteenth century when there was a Civil War in America. During that war, people in the Northern states who opposed the slave trade fought against people in the South who supported the right to have human chattels. Both sides claimed to support their argument with Scripture and both sides suffered enormously during the war. It may be stated that arguments in favour of slavery, as in the case of so many moral and ethical issues, are not supportable on scriptural grounds. Yet, should disagreement over the interpretation of Scripture keep one from bearing the burdens of others? Do the bonds of love in Christ call one to enter into the grief of others regardless of the cause of the pain? The point I am trying to make is that care must be taken not simply to speak of 'suffering together' or 'union in Christ' as if it can be easily embraced. Especially when suffering is the result of action which is justified on scriptural grounds, ethical and moral questions must be wrestled with if Christian spirituality is to be lived out in the world.

Many Christians today may argue that a stand for justice and freedom will lead to a greater identification with those who suffer as a result of their struggle for liberation. Yet it must also be argued that sharing in the bonds of Christ will call one to bear the burdens of grief of those who have been oppressed as well as those who are oppressors. By arguing that one must enter into the suffering of others I am not suggesting that one must offer support to oppression. Injustice should never be tolerated and lack of tolerance for others must always be opposed. Christian freedom, which finds its source in commitment to Christ stands solidly against oppression and injustice in any form. To take such a stand, of course, is to choose the way of suffering for the sake of Christ. This can be seen clearly, for instance, in the position taken by Oscar Romero, the archbishop of San Salvador who spoke out on behalf of the poor and as a result was assassinated on 24 March 1980. Romero consistently argued that God had placed the Church on the side of the poor and as a result could expect persecution.

> The church cannot do otherwise, for it remembers that Jesus had pity on the multitude. But by defending the poor it has entered into serious conflict with the powerful who belong to the monied oligarchies and with the political and military authorities of the state. This defense of the poor in a world deep in conflict has occasioned something new in the recent history of our church: persecution . . . Real persecution has been directed against the poor, the body of Christ in history today. They, like Jesus, are the crucified, the persecuted servant of Yahweh. They are the ones who make up in their own bodies that which is lacking in the passion of Christ.[30]

Yet, if one understands the covenant love of God in Christ, many Christians would argue that even while standing against injustice, Christians must continue to love their enemies. They do so because they believe that God's radical, vulnerable love finds its truest expression in following in the way of Christ who was willing to embrace suffering for others. This love still loves even those who continue to despise, ridicule and crucify. Commitment to Christ, crucified and risen, is a willingness to walk the road of suffering for the sake of Christ.

In addition to theological and doctrinal challenges to the idea of a suffering community, there are pressures within the social order that discourage a real relationship 'in Christ'. For example, western society often seems to stress individual need rather than communal concern. The western consumer society seems to encourage individuals to 'pick and choose' what will fit in with their schedule and plans, rather than seeing real sharing in Christ as part of the vocation of every believer. Care must be taken, of course, not to over-simplify the whole issue of sharing with others in suffering, particularly when thinking about relationship 'in Christ' on a larger regional, national or international scale. Indeed, it is possible to argue that while we speak of global relationships, in fact, distance, lack of personal contact, absence of meaningful communication – as well as the vastly different contexts in which we live – means that it isn't possible to 'share in' the sufferings of others in any significant way. Yet, it is also true that Christians believe that the love of Christ extends beyond all human boundaries of race, creed and geography. Indeed many Christians claim that through the suffering love of Christ, it is possible for all levels of diversity and difference to be drawn together into one. When Christians campaign or demonstrate, give charitable aid, offer prayers, write letters of protest, at some level this is not simply 'caring for' others, it is actually 'caring with' them.

This kind of sharing in the sufferings of others is expressed in the well-known prayer of St Francis of Assisi (1181–1226):

Lord, make me an instrument of your peace.
Where there is hatred, let me sow love,
Where there is injury, pardon;
Where there is doubt, faith;
Where there is despair, hope;
Where there is darkness, light;
Where there is sadness, joy.
O divine Master, grant that I may not so much seek
To be consoled, as to console,
To be understood, as to understand,
To be loved, as to love,
For it is in giving that we receive;
It is in pardoning that we are pardoned;
It is in dying that we are born to eternal life.[31]

St Francis' emphasis is on 'caring with' or participating in rather than 'caring for' others. Significantly, his emphasis on 'dying' and therefore 'finding' life highlights the fact that sharing in the 'sufferings of others' for the sake of Christ is the mark of true freedom in Christ. Four centuries later, Martin Luther would sum up this type of freedom – a freedom which comes from being bound to Christ – in his comment that: 'A Christian is a perfectly free lord of all, subject to none. A Christian is a dutiful servant of all, subject to all.'[32]

All of this discussion on the possibility of 'sharing in the suffering of Christ' may sound idealistic and far removed from the Christian churches many of us have known or observed. Yet the union that comes through deep relationship to Christ and participation in his sufferings is not built on acceptance of certain ideas about God. It is rather a real participation in relationship with Christ. Thus unity is not based on being forced to accept certain ideas, or adopt particular customs. Far from being a desire to 'save oneself' by trying to do good deeds or by keeping certain religious practices or by believing certain doctrines, Christian faith is about 'losing oneself' and all that a person might have considered important for the sake of Christ. The Apostle Paul, in writing to the Christians in Philippi, claimed that at one point he had much cause for boasting in his religious deeds and practices. Only when he was willing to put behind 'all that was past', and seek to share in the suffering of Christ did he discover the joy and freedom that relationship with Christ brings (Philippians 3.4–11).

What Paul was describing here was not something that he had fully realized. He was speaking of the aim or goal of the Christian's calling. Claiming that he wanted to know Christ and share in his sufferings, he wrote:

> Not that I have already obtained this or have reached the goal; but I press on to make it my own, because Christ Jesus has made me his own. Beloved, I do not consider that I have made it my own; but this one thing I do: forgetting what lies behind and straining forward to what lies ahead, I press on toward the goal of the prize of the heavenly call of God in Christ Jesus (Philippians 3.12–14).

The idea of pressing on toward the goal of a heavenly prize leads us to an exploration of the idea of the way people understand the aim or purpose of the Christian. For some the goal is a new community in heaven, for others it is about a way of being in relationship here on earth too. While Christians differ in the way they think it will find expression, most hope for a sight of the 'new heaven' and the 'new earth' promised in Scripture (Revelation 21.1). The promise and the hope of a new community is the subject of the final chapter.

Draw your own conclusions

Reflect on the idea of suffering as 'choice'. What difference does it make to say that suffering is central to Christian spirituality?

What do you think it means to share in the sufferings of others for the sake of Christ? How might shared suffering find expression today?

Christian faith claims that followers of Christ are to love their enemies. How is it possible to love both the oppressed and the oppressor?

Further reading

On the Christian doctrine of the atonement

Gustav Aulén (1931), *Christus Victor, An Historical Study of the Three Main Types of the Idea of the Atonement*, tr. A. G. Herbert, New York: Macmillan.

Paul S. Fiddes (1988/1992), *The Creative Suffering of God*, Oxford: Clarendon Press.

Paul S. Fiddes (1989), *Past Event and Present Salvation: The Christian Idea of Atonement*, London: Darton, Longman & Todd.

Stanley Hauerwas (1990), *Naming the Silences*, Grand Rapids: William Eerdmans.

S. Mark Heim (2006), *Saved From Sacrifice, A Theology of the Cross*, Grand Rapids: William Eerdmanns.

C. S. Lewis (2001), *The Problem of Pain*, New York: HarperCollins.

Arthur McGill (1982), *Suffering: A Test of Theological Method*, Philadelphia: Westminster Press.

Stephen Sykes (1997), *The Story of Atonement*, London: Darton, Longman & Todd.

Miroslav Volf (2005), *Giving and Forgiving in a Culture Stripped of Grace*, Grand Rapids: Zondervan.

J. Denny Weaver (2001), *The Nonviolent Atonement*, Grand Rapids: William Eerdmans.

Philip Yancey (1990), *Where is God When it Hurts?*, Grand Rapids: Zondervan.

Notes

1 John V. Taylor (1986), *Weep Not For Me: Meditations on the Cross and the Resurrection*, Geneva: World Council of Churches, p. 12.

2 Jürgen Moltmann (1974), *The Crucified God: The Cross of Christ as the Foundation and Criticism of Christian Theology*, trans. R. A. Wilson and J. Bowden, London: SCM Press.

3 John Macquarrie (1977), *Principles of Christian Theology*, 2nd edn, New York: Charles Scribner's Sons, p. 256.

4 Rowan Williams (2003), *The Dwelling of the Light: Praying With Icons of Christ*, Norwich: Canterbury Press, p. 19.

5 For a discussion of some of these issues see Paul S. Fiddes (2000), *Participating in God: A Pastoral Doctrine of the Trinity*, London: Darton, Longman & Todd, pp. 152ff.

6 Flora Slosson Wuellner (1989), 'When Prayer Encounters Pain', in The

Wound of Our Mortality, *Weavings, A Journal of the Christian Spiritual Life*, May/June, IV, no. 3, p. 34.

7 Wuellner, 'When Prayer Encounters Pain', p. 34.

8 Wuellner, 'When Prayer Encounters Pain', p. 36.

9 Wuellner, 'When Prayer Encounters Pain', p. 36.

10 Wuellner, 'When Prayer Encounters Pain', p. 35.

11 John Newton (1779), 'How Sweet the Name of Jesus Sounds', in *Baptist Praise and Worship* (1991), Oxford: Oxford University Press.

12 Gordon Mursell (2001), *English Spirituality from Earliest Times to 1700*, London/Louisville: Westminster John Knox Press, pp. 159ff.

13 Mursell, *English Spirituality*, pp. 161–2.

14 Julian of Norwich (1987), *Revelations of Divine Love*, ed. Halcyon Backhouse, London: Hodder & Stoughton, p. 62.

15 Julian of Norwich, *Revelations*, p. 62.

16 Julian of Norwich, *Revelations*, p. 63.

17 John V. Taylor (1986), *A Matter of Life and Death*, London: SCM Press, pp. 46–7.

18 Taylor, *Life and Death*, p. 46.

19 Julian of Norwich, *Revelations*, pp. 46–7.

20 Dietrich Bonhoeffer (1948/1959), *The Cost of Discipleship*, London: SCM Press, p. 79.

21 Bonhoeffer, *Discipleship*, pp. 78, 80.

22 Bonhoeffer, *Discipleship*, p. 82.

23 Morna D. Hooker (1991), *The Gospel According to St Mark*, Black's New Testament Commentaries, London: A&C Black, p. 22.

24 Diary of Anne Cator Steele, 1 April 1734. The Angus Library, Regent's Park College, Oxford.

25 Origen, 'Exhortation to Martyrdom', as cited in Boniface Ramsey (1986), *Beginning to Read the Fathers*, London: Darton, Longman & Todd, p. 131.

26 Nicholas Wolterstorff (1989), *Lament for a Son*, London: Hodder & Stoughton, p. 56.

27 Eduard Schweizer (1971/1981), *The Good News According to Mark*, London: SPCK, pp. 221–2.

28 Pierre Teilhard de Chardin (1965/1970), *Hymn of the Universe*, London: Collins, p. 109.

29 Douglas Steere (1984), *Quaker Spirituality: Selected Writings*, London: SPCK.

30 Oscar Romero (1980), 'The Political Dimension of the Faith from the Perspective of the Poor', in Andrew Bradstock and Christopher Rowland (eds) (2002), *Radical Christian Writings, A Reader*, Oxford: Blackwell, pp. 278–9.

31 'Prayer by St Francis of Assisi', in George Appleton (ed.) (1985), *The Oxford Book of Prayer*, Oxford: Oxford University Press, p. 75.

32 Martin Luther, 'Freedom of A Christian', in John Dillenberger (ed.) (1961), *Martin Luther: Selections From His Writings*, Garden City, New York: Doubleday/Anchor, p. 53.

6

Dreaming of a New Community

If you had one wish what would it be? Surrounded by the devastation of civil war and poverty, the woman looked down at the ground and then back up and stared out at me from my television screen and said, 'I want my children to live in a different world. I long for a world I have never known.' I have never forgotten her words or the way she said them. She was dreaming of a new community.

Even those who have never had to face the crippling effects of un-treated disease or hunger may understand this longing. It may be a desire for a world that doesn't glamorize wealth or encourage greed; one that doesn't rejoice in wrong, but celebrates truth and justice. This longing for a 'different world' is at the heart of Christian spirituality. It is described in different ways: sometimes it is understood as the kingdom of God on earth. At other times it is described as the kingdom beyond, like a 'heavenly home'. Both of the views of eschatology (teaching of the last things) have shaped Christian spirituality and the way one expresses the longing for a new world.

Biblical views of a different world order

The Old Testament prophet Isaiah longed for a new day and imagined what it would be like when God's way was established on earth. He wrote of a new kingdom, or perhaps we might call it a new community which would be characterized by genuine peace (*shalom*). The vision is of a new community when all things in the whole created earth will be at one. As the biblical writer describes it, on that day many nations will come together to the Lord that he 'may teach us his ways and that we may walk in his paths'. Then the prophet continues: 'they shall beat their swords into plough-shares, and their spears into pruning hooks; nation shall not lift up sword against nation, neither shall they learn war anymore' (Isaiah 2.2–4).

In another place, this is pictured as a new heaven and a new earth, a sort of peaceable kingdom where the 'wolf and the lamb shall feed together' (Isaiah 65.17–25). A day when the Lord would wipe away the tears from all faces and the whole of creation would sing for joy:

The wilderness and the dry land shall be glad, the desert shall rejoice and blossom; like the crocus it shall blossom abundantly, and rejoice with joy and singing . . . Then the eyes of the blind shall be opened, and the ears of the deaf unstopped; then the lame shall leap like a deer, and the tongue of the speechless sing for joy. For waters shall break forth in the wilderness, and streams in the desert; the burning sand shall become a pool and the thirsty ground springs of water . . . A highway shall be there, and it shall be called the Holy Way; the unclean shall not travel on it, but it shall be for God's people; no traveller, not even fools shall go astray. No lion shall be there, nor shall any ravenous beast come up on it; they shall not be found there, but the redeemed shall walk there. And the ransomed of the Lord shall return, and come to Zion with singing; everlasting joy shall be upon their heads; they shall obtain joy and gladness, and sorrow and sighing shall flee away. (Isaiah 35.1–10)

It is a vision of peace, which focuses on a time when God's people will come home to God and there will be a new world order. But when will the day arrive? When will the vision be a reality? Those were the questions asked many times by the people of God, as the prophets described the arrival of a wonderful day.

Originally, the vision seems to have been applied to the Jews who were in exile in Babylon and later perhaps included the Jews of the Diaspora. Christians, though, have read the Old Testament texts as a vision of the kingdom of God which was announced with the coming of Jesus. The Gospel writers saw the coming of Jesus as the beginning of a new era. They announced that in Jesus, the kingdom of God had dawned. Yet since there was no firm agreement on how the reign of God was, or would be, made visible, Christians have interpreted the unfolding of God's purposes (his reign) in different ways: waiting in expectant hope or taking action or sometimes a combining of the two. For instance, some Christians believe that while 'the kingdom of God' was announced by Jesus, we are still waiting to see it and it will happen in an instant. They see the world as a bad place which we need to be 'saved from' and often focus on the need to wait expectantly for the bodily return of Christ to earth. The idea is that Christ will come in judgement, without warning: like a 'thief in the night' or in the 'twinkling of an eye' (Luke 12.35–40). Others feel God's kingdom will appear more slowly, almost like a drama that is being played out, as there is a gradual unfolding of God's purposes. These may wait expectantly to see what God will do, while others feel it is their responsibility actively to co-operate with God in the drama.

For Christians who hold to a view that the kingdom was begun in the ministry of Jesus, but will not be fulfilled until some later time in the future, there is a very clear sense of both the 'now and the not yet'. For some this means that we live now and wait for the day when we will die and 'go to heaven'. For them, the kingdom may be ultimately a heavenly place where all of God's faithful will be gathered together. Still others who have a clear sense of the 'now and the not yet' believe that the kingdom will be, or perhaps better is already being, realized here on earth. For those who hold this view, there is a belief that the new world which is so longed for is being created day by day and we may participate in bringing it about. They believe that the kingdom may be ushered in by us as we change our minds, ways and attitudes. It happens one person at a time, one life at a time, one day at a time. It is about joining our 'love energies' with the 'love energy of God'.[1] For Christians who hold this view, there is an emphasis on waiting in order to see all that God longs to do, but there is also a very real sense in which even now Christians must join our longings with God's longings and indeed the longing of all creation to bring in the kingdom here on earth. When these Christians pray in the words of the Lord's prayer, 'your kingdom come your will be done', they feel it is their responsibility to live out that prayer in action.

Over the years Christian views on the kingdom of God have been as varied as the number of Christians and it would be impossible here to describe the many and mixed understandings of eschatological hope (expectation based on belief in the last things). What perhaps is most important to note is that all Christians would describe some sense of longing for a different world or a new community. Moreover, in some way all would recognize the need at times for both waiting and action. The way that these two features, both waiting and action, are combined will often determine the pattern of spirituality that emerges at a particular time.

Henri Nouwen claimed that once a friend wrote to him and said: 'learning to weep, learning to keep vigil, learning to wait for the dawn. Perhaps this is what it means to be human.'[2] Most people have waited: for new relationships when old friends have been left behind or for courage to live through grief. Nouwen was right; it is a universal experience, it is 'part of what it means to be human' to wait: if we live, we wait, and at times we weep and keep vigil.

Waiting is often difficult on a human level. No one likes to wait either in anticipation or in dread of an event. Yet the waiting moments that are significant to Christian spirituality are not related to simply watching the passing of time or waiting for an event in time. Rather the waiting which is at the heart of Christian spirituality is linked to longing and desire and specifically to the hope of a different world.

Biblical views on waiting

The idea of 'waiting on the Lord' may be found throughout the pages of Scripture. Most notably the Psalmist often spoke of the need to wait on the Lord. Psalm 38 includes this comment: 'O Lord, all my longing is known to you; my sighing is not hidden from you. My heart throbs, my strength fails me . . . But it is for you, O Lord, that I wait' (vv. 9, 15). Psalm 39 says: 'And now, O Lord, what do I wait for? My hope is in you' (v. 7). And Psalm 40 includes this affirmation: 'I waited patiently for the Lord; he inclined to me and heard my cry' (v. 1). There are many other references in the Bible to waiting on the Lord. However, this is not, metaphorically speaking, the 'twiddling of thumbs' or 'wringing of hands' while wishing that something might happen. This is not an empty sort of waiting. Rather there is a real sense in which Christians are to wait in hopeful expectation. This expectancy is based on the assurance that just as God has acted in the past, so one expects God to act in the future. It is not passive, but active waiting. It may be likened to the idea of waiting for something to grow. Like a seed that has been planted we wait for it to spring forth. This waiting involves looking and hoping and yearning and longing for all that God has promised to do. Jesus explained this kind of waiting in parables about seed being planted and growing. He said:

'The Kingdom of God is as if someone would scatter seed on the ground, and would sleep and rise night and day, and the seed would sprout and grow, he does not know how. The earth produces of itself, first the stalk, then the head, then the full grain in the head. But when the grain is ripe, at once he goes in with his sickle because the harvest has come . . . With what can we compare the kingdom of God, or what parable will we use for it? It is like a mustard seed, which, when sown upon the ground, is the smallest of all the seeds on earth; yet when it is sown it grows up and becomes the greatest of all shrubs, and puts forth large branches, so that the birds of the air can make nests in its shade.' (Mark 4.26–32)

In this parable, there is very real sense of expectation and hope. It is the expectation that while human beings may not be able to see or to recognize all that God is doing, God is at work, often in quiet, almost unnoticed ways. Christian faith teaches that just as one cannot see a seed growing, so we cannot see all that God will one day reveal. So for now, Christians believe that they actively wait, that is, as the Apostle Paul put it, they join with the whole of creation in 'eager longing' (Romans 8.19), believing that God as love will see love's purposes through. Christians wait, depending on God as Holy Spirit to interpret our deepest longings with sighs too deep for words (Romans 8.26). Christian faith teaches that in relationship with God and one another, Christians are called to wait and trust in God. And waiting can only be active for it is the waiting of participation in relationship with God who has gone before, walks beside and shall come behind, too.

In his book, *The Stature of Waiting*, V. H. Vanstone pointed out that waiting patiently in expectation is at the heart of the understanding of the passion of Christ. Central to the story of Jesus' passion, according to Vanstone, is that Jesus was 'handed over'.[3] Pointing out that the first part of Jesus' ministry was filled with activity as he went about preaching and teaching, he notes that when it came to the passion narratives, he was found waiting. In the place called Gethsemane, he was praying and longing for a different way into the future. He was, one might say, longing for a different world. But immediately after he was handed over, he could only wait as things were being done to him. He was arrested and questioned, he was mocked and spat upon, he was nailed to the cross, he was crowned with thorns, he could only wait to die.

Vanstone suggests that when Jesus said 'it is accomplished', he did not mean as some have suggested that he had finished all he had wanted to do. Rather, he meant that he had waited and allowed things to be done to him in order to fulfil his vocation. In commenting on Vanstone's ideas, Henri Nouwen suggests that 'Jesus' passion was a kind of waiting'. Moreover Nouwen claims: 'Here we glimpse the mystery of God's incarnation. God became human so we could act upon God and God could be the recipient of our responses.'[4] All action, according to Vanstone, ends in passion because the response to our action is out of our hands. In the end, 'it is part of the mystery of work, of friendship, of community, that they always involve waiting'.[5]

Active waiting

The idea of waiting as part of our participation in the passion of Christ is a theme in many of the Christian devotional writings. Reflecting on the suffering of Christ, Evelyn Underhill suggests that just as 'the Lord's quiet time was Gethsemane' so we must have moments when we wait before 'making a great spiritual effort'. She argues that Christians must reflect on the pain and conflict Christ faced, and then recognize:

Weariness and desolation of spirit, the complete disappearance of everything that could minister to spiritual self-love, humiliating falls and bitter deprivations, the apparent failure even of faith, buffetings of Satan renewed when least expected . . .[6]

All of this and more, according to Underhill, is part of the Christian way. Having reflected on the struggle, the Christian is then called to respond, though the way may be difficult. She writes:

> Little wonder that the Christian must be sturdy about it; fit for all weathers, and indifferent to his interior ups and downs. Umbrellas, mackintoshes and digestive tabloids are not issued to genuine travellers on this way. Comfort and safety-first must give place to courage and love, if we are to become – as we should be – the travelling agents of the Divine Charity. If the road on which we find ourselves is narrow, with bad surfaces and many sudden gradients, it is probably the right route. The obvious and convenient by-pass which skirts the worst hill also by-passes the city set upon the hill: the City of the Contemplation of the love of God. It gives a very nice general view to the pious motorist; but those who enter the City must put up with the bad approach. After a certain point the right road is marked 'unfit for motors', and the traveller must go forward alone.[7]

Underhill's reminder is that after a time of 'quiet' one might then journey, albeit through difficulty, in order to discover life with God. It also seems that there was a realization that even as individuals withdrew to wait they would find that they discovered a whole new way of perceiving themselves and the world. Thomas Kelly, for instance, suggests that:

> we are torn loose from earthly attachments and ambitions – *contemptus mundi*. And we are quickened to divine but painful concern for the world – *amor mundi*. He plucks the world out of our hearts, loosening the chains of attachment. He hurls the world into our hearts, where we and he together carry it in infinitely tender love.[8]

Kelly meant that the kind of waiting that comes from prayer and silent attentiveness means that we 'learn to live in the passive voice', as we actively wait for life 'to be willed through' us.[9]

A recognition that active waiting is part of life in Christ is a reminder that just because we wait does not mean that everything will be 'put right' as we understand it. In other words if, as was discussed in Chapter 5, one waits in the belief that in being united with Christ one is united to others in suffering, sometimes a person may wait in the midst of pain and in the knowledge that our current circumstances or those of others cannot be changed.

I was nine years of age, when a lovely woman who was a children's worker in my church did not come to our Bible group one week and we were told that her husband had died tragically when his car had collided with a train. We didn't see her for several weeks and when she did return, we gathered our chairs in a circle around her in the usual way in order for her to tell us the Bible story. As she began to speak, suddenly she began to cry. I remember quite vividly sitting there as part of a little group of youngsters gathered around a teacher, silent and waiting. I also remember how I wished that I could do something to help her and to somehow put things right for her. Many years later, I realized that although we were only a group of children, we were probably doing all anyone could do for her that night; we were waiting with her.

The idea of waiting is not something that human beings find easy to embrace. Yet while action is often promoted by culture, at times we are to wait. As we do we listen and yearn and hope and catch a glimpse of a world to be. A world which we are sometimes prompted to work toward and speak for, but ultimately a world which is not of our making, but a sign of the transforming power of the Spirit. And the challenge for Christians is to listen with 'eager longing' and, with expectancy, to wait on the Lord.

Acting on a vision of a new community

In many ways because the vision of community reflects something of the very nature of God who is community, we find that the vision is forever changing and forming, as we grow closer to God and to one another. Yet it is the task of community, when prompted, to act on the vision which has been given. We realize, of course, that in our search for God, the vision for community may change; indeed, it is always being transformed by God, who by means of the power at work within us is able to do far more abundantly than we could ever ask of or think (Ephesians 3.20). Yet day by day we are called to join our love energies with the love energies of God so that God's purposes may be revealed in our life together.

There are many examples from Christian history of those who have given themselves to a vision of new community. We will explore the spirituality of two individuals: a Roman Catholic, Dorothy Day and a Baptist, Martin Luther King Jr.

Dorothy Day

When Dorothy Day died at the age of 83 on 29 November 1980, *Newsweek* magazine reported that she had been 'perhaps the most influential Catholic of her time'.[10] Founder of *The Catholic Worker*, a monthly tabloid newspaper, Day felt called to live and work among the poor. In her autobiography, she described her life in a way that can only be explained as being driven by desire. Borrowing from the words of Mary Ward (1585–1645), Day described her restlessness as a 'long loneliness'. She wrote 'We have all known the long loneliness, and we have learned that the only solution is love and that love comes with community.'[11]

Born in Brooklyn, New York on 8 November 1897, she later lived with her family in California and experienced the devastation of the San Francisco earthquake before her family moved back to a tenement flat in Chicago. After her father was appointed a sports editor of a Chicago newspaper, they moved to a more comfortable house on the north side of town. However, Day never forgot the plight of the poor and dispossessed.

She won a scholarship to the University of Illinois in the autumn of 1914, but dropped out of university two years later and moved to New York where she found a job as a reporter for *The Call*, the city's socialist paper. She then worked for *The Masses*, a magazine that opposed American involvement in the war in Europe. In November 1917 Day went to prison for protesting against political arrests with 40 other women in front of the White House. After 15 days in jail and participation in a hunger strike, she was released. However, she became more and more convinced that the social order was unjust and that she must work to try to change it.

From childhood, Day had gathered some impressions of the Catholic Church. Her parents did not regularly attend a church, but Day recalled hearing stories from a friend about the lives of the saints and perhaps, most significantly, she was impressed when she saw her neighbour, Mrs Barret, on her knees praying. She claimed that for a time she herself began to pray at night, kneeling until her 'knees ached' and she was 'cold and stiff'.[12] These early notions about the Christian faith did not last and she eventually turned from belief in God, claiming that she did not see many Christians living out the radical call of the gospel. Those Christians who did seem to care for the poor, like the Salvation Army, did not appeal to her. She wrote:

> I wanted life and I wanted the abundant life. I wanted it for others too. I did not want just the few, missionary-minded people like the

Salvation Army, to be kind to the poor, as the poor. I wanted everyone to be kind. I wanted every home to be open to the lame, the halt and the blind . . .[13]

Her concern for the poor led her to join the Socialist Party when she was a student at the University of Illinois. While she was a student, she found room and board with a family who attended the Methodist church. Day claimed that even as 'I talked about religion I rejected religion'.[14] She became very critical of religious people who seemed at ease with life while others faced dire poverty. Later, as a young journalist, she continued to feel that her place was among the poor and she began to participate actively in protests, even going to jail, because of her stand against the injustices within society.

Between 1917 and 1918, as the war raged in Europe and influenza broke out at home, she decide to support the war effort without compromising her pacifist views, by working as a nurse in a hospital. The work was very tiring and while she still did not openly profess a belief in God, she found herself attending early morning Mass with a friend on a Sunday and drawing strength from the experience of worship. After this brief stint at nursing, she returned to her work as a journalist and at times she would make late-night visits to St Joseph's church on Sixth Avenue in New York. She knew little of Catholic belief, but saw the Church as a church of the immigrants, the Church of the poor. It was during this period that she later recalled how she would meet Eugene O'Neill in a bar in Greenwich village and he would recite to her the 'The Hound of Heaven' by Francis Thompson. Perhaps it was then that she began to believe that the hound of heaven would never stop baying at her heels, nor would the long loneliness cease, as long as there were people who were being treated unjustly.

By 1924, Day was living in a beach cottage on Staten Island and began a common law marriage with Forster Batterham, a biologist she had met through friends in Manhattan. Batterham did not share Day's belief in God and as her conviction of God's love and care for the world began to grow, their relationship began to fracture. He could not understand Day's 'absorption with the supernatural'. Although he did not believe in God, Day claimed that 'it was life with him that brought me natural happiness, that brought me to God'.[15] She looked back on those years as a time of great joy, yet she described the peace she found as being 'divided against itself'. She wrote:

It was peace, curiously enough, divided against itself. I was happy but my very happiness made me know that there was a greater happiness to be obtained from life than any I had ever known. I began to think, to weigh things, and it was at this time that I began consciously to pray more.[16]

A turning point came when Day became pregnant and on 3 March 1927, Tamar Teresa Day was born. Day was overwhelmed with gratitude and out of a desire to express her thanks to God, she began to think about baptism for the child. Batterham was against her Christian belief and she knew that if she persisted in it, her relationship with him would end. In spite of the deep joy of relationship between mother and child, she knew that there was a longing within which would not be stilled. She wrote:

Yet always those deep moments of happiness gave way to a feeling of struggle, of a long silent fight still to be gone through. There had been the physical struggle, the mortal combat almost, of giving birth to a child, and now there was coming the struggle for my own soul. Tamar would be baptized and I knew the rending it would cause in human relations around me. I was to be torn and agonized again, and I was all for putting off the hard day.[17]

Tamar's baptism and Day's own conversion to Catholicism marked a permanent break with Batterham. Dorothy Day then began a lifelong journey in which she would combine her radical social views with a deep and abiding faith in the living Christ. In the beginning she was not sure how she could do this. She wrote of this period in her life that she felt that after becoming a Catholic she had not done enough to help others.

How little, how puny my work had been since becoming a Catholic, I thought. How self-centered, how ingrown, how lacking in sense of community! My summer of quiet reading and prayer, my self-absorption seemed sinful as I watched my brothers in their struggle, not for themselves but for others.[18]

In the winter of 1932, she went to Washington DC as a reporter for several magazines to report on a hunger march. She watched protestors parade down the streets of Washington carrying signs calling for jobs, unemployment insurance, old-age pensions, relief for mothers and children's health care and housing. What kept her from joining the march was that it had been organized by Communists and as a Catholic she felt she should not join with them. After witnessing the march Day said she prayed: 'I offered up a special prayer, prayer which came with tears and with anguish, that some way would open up for me to use what talents I possessed for my fellow workers, for the poor.'[19]

Back in her apartment, the next day, she met Peter Maurin, a French immigrant who had adopted a Franciscan attitude toward life, living a life of prayer and embracing poverty as a vocation. He had a vision for a new social order built upon the teaching of the Gospels. George Shuster, the editor of *The Commonweal* magazine, which Day had worked for, had given Maurin her address. For Day the meeting was an answer to prayer and when Maurin encouraged her to start a paper to publicize Catholic social teaching to promote steps to bring about a new society, Day readily embraced the idea. *The Catholic Worker* was born and soon 100,000 copies were being printed and distributed. The paper was a voice for change; it challenged the values of society and called people to actively seek to bring about change.

Soon Day and Maurin found that people were beginning to come to them for help and volunteers who wanted to make a difference began to knock on the door. Maurin's essays in *The Catholic Worker* called for people to practise hospitality and reach out to friend and stranger. Day's own apartment became the first of a number of houses of hospitality. For Day, the motivation was love. And for her, love meant a real identification with the poor and the downcast. She did not simply care for them: she lived with them and among them as an expression of her passion.

Not everyone appreciated the kind of openness that Day showed to others. Some claimed that the people she took in were not all 'deserving poor'. A visiting social worker asked Day how long the 'clients' were permitted to stay. 'We let them stay forever,' Day answered, 'they live with us, they die with us, and we give them a Christian burial. We pray for them after they are dead. Once they are taken in they become members of the family. Or rather they always were members of the family. They are our brothers and sisters in Christ.'[20]

Love in Christ, or rather for Day, love in action, was at the heart of her approach to spirituality. This was participation in God: love in action was to be shown within both the community of believers and the wider community around her. To sustain her in her work, daily she 'waited on the Lord' as she meditated on Scripture: prayer was part of the daily pattern of life. Furthermore, she had a very strong sacramental sense of life, turning daily to the celebration of the Eucharist for sustenance. But she also saw that the whole of life was filled with the love of God. While life could be hard, she believed that love in action could win through.

There is much more which could be said about Day, but what seems clear from all her writing and work for peace and social justice is that she held firmly to a vision for a different kind of world order. Whatever happened, she believed that love – the love known in community – was the answer. The Catholic Worker Movement was built on the idea that Christian faith is relational – it is about loving God and loving people. For it to be relational, she believed it must be seen in community while at the same time drawing the lines of community ever wider until it finally embraced all. This was nothing short of a revolution of the heart which she described in this way:

> The greatest challenge of the day is: how to bring about a revolution of the heart, a revolution which has to start with each one of us? When we begin to take the lowest place, to wash the feet of others, to love our brothers with that burning love, that passion, which led to the Cross, then we can truly say, 'Now I have begun.'[21]

Dorothy Day's dream of a new community was based on the belief that if she waited expectantly and worked diligently, one day God's kingdom would come on earth even as it was in heaven. Day was fond of citing the example of Thérèse of Lisieux (1873–97), a member of the Carmelite order, who claimed that 'little by little' God's love would be made known. Day's desire for a different kind of world also led her to support the work of other Christians who longed for a different world. Among them the outspoken Baptist minister, Martin Luther King, Jr who became a leader in the Civil Rights movement in America.

Martin Luther King, Jr

Born in Atlanta, Georgia, on 29 January 1929, Martin Luther King, Jr was the son of schoolteacher Alberta Williams King and Baptist minister Martin Luther King, Sr.[22] As a youngster, his keen intellectual gifts became obvious and he went on to graduate from Morehouse College in 1948 and then from Crozer Theological Seminary in 1951. He completed his PhD at Boston University in 1955. He married Coretta Scott King in 1953 and in 1954 they moved to Montgomery, Alabama, where he became the pastor of Dexter Avenue Baptist Church. As an African-American, King had grown up knowing the cruelty of a segregated culture and as he looked on the plight of the people, and realized the bonds holding both the oppressed and the oppressor, King found himself drawn into a life of non-violent protest against social injustice.

King joined with other African-American ministers to form the Southern Christian Leadership Conference in 1957, which advocated the use of non-violent civil disobedience in order to gain equal rights for all citizens in America. As the first president of the movement, King began speaking, writing and leading others to join in protest. In his speeches, he constantly put before others the dream of a new community, a new world order. In a well-known speech King declared:

I say to you today, my friends, so even though we face the difficulties of today and tomorrow, I still have a dream. It is a dream deeply rooted in the American dream. I have a dream that one day this nation will rise up and live out the true meaning of its creed: 'We hold these truths to be self-evident: that all men are created equal.' I have a dream that one day on the red hills of Georgia the sons of former slaves and the sons of former slave owners will be able to sit down together at the table of brotherhood. I have a dream that one day even the state of Mississippi, a state sweltering with the heat of injustice, sweltering with the heat of oppression, will be transformed into an oasis of freedom and justice. I have a dream that my four little children will one day live in a nation where they will not be judged by the colour of their skin but by the content of their character.

I have a dream today. I have a dream that one day, down in Alabama, with its vicious racists, with its governor having his lips dripping with the words of interposition and nullification; one day right there in Alabama, little black boys and black girls will be able to join hands with little white boys and white girls as sisters and brothers.

I have a dream today. I have a dream that one day every valley shall be exalted, every hill and mountain shall be made low, the rough places will be made plain, and the crooked places will be made straight, and the glory of the Lord shall be revealed, and all flesh shall see it together. This is our hope. This is the faith that I go back to the South with. With this faith we will be able to hew out of the mountain of despair a stone of hope. With this faith we will be able to transform the jangling discords of our nation into a beautiful symphony of brotherhood. With this faith we will be able to work together, to pray together, to struggle together, to go to jail together, to stand up for freedom together, knowing that we will be free one day.

This will be the day when all of God's children will be able to sing with a new meaning, 'My country, 'tis of thee, sweet land of liberty, of thee I sing. Land where my fathers died, land of the pilgrim's pride, from every mountainside, let freedom ring.' And if America is to be a great nation this must become true. So let freedom ring from the prodigious hilltops of New Hampshire. Let freedom ring from the mighty mountains of New York. Let freedom ring from the heightening Alleghenies of Pennsylvania!

Let freedom ring from the snowcapped Rockies of Colorado!

Let freedom ring from the curvaceous slopes of California!

But not only that; let freedom ring from Stone Mountain of Georgia!

Let freedom ring from Lookout Mountain of Tennessee!

Let freedom ring from every hill and molehill of Mississippi. From every mountainside, let freedom ring.

And when this happens, when we allow freedom to ring, when we let it ring from every village and every hamlet, from every state and every city, we will be able to speed up that day when all of God's children, black men and white men, Jews and Gentiles, Protestants and Catholics, will be able to join hands and sing in the words of the old Negro spiritual, 'Free at last! Free at last! Thank God Almighty, we are free at last!'[23]

King's words captivated the hearts and minds of many people. He readily acknowledged, of course, that he himself had been influenced by the non-violent approach of Mahatma Gandhi, nurtured by his own reading of Scripture, and shaped by the theological views of people like the nineteenth-century advocate of the Social Gospel movement, Walter Rauschenbusch. A Baptist pastor to a congregation in Hell's Kitchen in New York, Rauschenbusch wrote several books, including *Christianity in Social Crisis*, in which he urged people to realize that sin was not simply a personal issue which was confined to the individual, but that sin was also part of the entire social order. For Rauschenbusch, Christian faith could never be relegated to a personal religion, since it was in every aspect social. The kingdom of God was 'not a matter of getting individuals to heaven, but of transforming the life on earth into the harmony of heaven'.[24]

King's assessment of the evils of segregation was shaped by these ideas and his own understanding that love was the only response to be made in the face of the evil of racism. King spoke eloquently of the need to meet hatred with love and of his belief that love would win through. Reflecting on his experience of participating in the Montgomery bus boycott, for instance, King said that living through the actual experience of protest reinforced his conviction that 'non-violence became more than a method to which I gave intellectual assent; it became a commitment to a way of life'.[25] What he learned through such experiences was that:

The non-violent approach does not immediately change the heart of the oppressor. It first does something to the hearts and souls of those committed to it. It gives them new self respect; it calls up resources of strength and courage that they did not know they had. Finally it reaches the opponent and so stirs his (or her) conscience that reconciliation becomes a reality.[26]

King, like Dorothy Day, clung to a vision of a new kind of community. He had a dream of the day when all people would sit together around one table. It was a vision of the kingdom. Reflecting on King's spirituality, E. Glenn Hinson has said that King realized that God's love energies can transform energies of hate into energies of God's peace.[27] Such transformation doesn't happen overnight. It is part of an ongoing process as people join together in community and abandon themselves to God. King's vision of community, centred on the belief that suffering is part of redemptive love, is reflected in his paraphrase of the words of Gandhi:

We will match your capacity to inflict suffering by our capacity to endure suffering. We shall meet your physical force with soul force. We will not hate you, but we cannot in all good conscience obey your unjust law. Do to us what you will and we will still love you. Bomb our homes and threaten our children; send your hooded perpetrators of violence into our communities and drag us out on some wayside road, beating us and leaving us half dead, and we will still love you. But we will soon wear you down by our capacity to suffer. And in winning our freedom we will so appeal to your heart and conscience that we will win you in the process.[28]

The vision of new community which is reflected in the life and work of Martin Luther King, Jr and Dorothy Day is not of a community that is free from pain and suffering. Moreover, the vision of community has nothing to do with a community that is shaped merely by images of success or power. Real community cannot thrive in places where people gather simply with those who seem like them in status and wealth and position. The vision is not simply to do with helping others; handouts from a position of power will never reveal the fullness of love. Nor is community about escapism or the idea that one can flee from the world and form a tight-knit group which will offer security. Rather this is a vision of community based on love which calls people, beckons them and pleads with them to engage actively with the struggles of the world and to strive to be channels of God's grace in order to participate in a new world order.

The work of King and Day call people to ponder the meaning of relationship with God and one another, in a way which is beyond community, as we presently know it. For both, there was a sense in which they glimpsed the hope of community which Christians believe is ultimately promised by Scripture – a place where there is no more night – no more tears, no more sorrow and sighing. In Christian thinking, it is recognized that Christians realize that such a community is little more than a vision as yet. However, if there is the willingness to actively wait, in abandonment to the love of God, then Christians believe that ultimately God's kingdom will be realized on earth even as it is in heaven.

Communion in the life of God

In speaking about the Christian faith, we have already acknowledged that sometimes it sounds as if people are only interested in the afterlife. That is to say, some Christians speak about life in Christ as if the only thing that matters is what happens after death. Both Day and King remind us that life in relationship with God and others is not simply about the hereafter, but is also about the here and now – or rather it is about the now and the not yet! In fact, there is a sense in which the two have merged and from time to time Christians are very aware of the closeness of the communion between the living and those who have physically died but still live in Christ. Even so, the whole idea of the communion of saints is a great mystery to most Christians. While in some traditions there is a very vital rhythm of marking the lives of the saints and honouring deep relationship by praying to and for the dead, in other traditions there are different ways (such as a plaque on the church wall) to remember the contribution of the saints who have gone before us and who still live to give praise and honour to God. In the Letter to the Hebrews, the writer pictures the believers who are seeking to live the Christian life, doing so within the full view of those who have gone before. He says it is as if they are running a race with the spectators gathered like a cloud of witnesses to watch and so he exhorts:

> Therefore, since we are surrounded by so great a cloud of witnesses, let us lay aside every weight and sin that clings so closely, and let us run with perseverance the race that is set before us, looking to Jesus the pioneer and perfecter of our faith, who for the sake of the joy that was set before him endured the cross, disregarding its shame, and has taken his seat at the right hand of the throne of God (Hebrews 12.1–2).

By acknowledging the communion of saints, Christians are simply recognizing the greater community in God to which all are called to participate. Kingdom goals embrace heaven and earth, as even now there may be the opportunity for those on earth to join their love energies with those of the wider community and with God's. Through prayer and worship there are moments when Christians affirm that the veil between this world and the next is very thin indeed.

My grandmother died in December 1998. During her 98 years on earth she had experienced the highs and lows of human experience. She had known disappointment and heartache. She had lived through the economic Depression of 1929 and when she was in her later 70s she and my grandfather lost most of their worldly goods in a fire which broke out after their home was struck by lightning. Toward the end of her life 'Mawmaw' grew increasingly frustrated with poor health mainly because her frail body would not respond to her active and alert mind. The week before she died, she was put into hospital and my grandfather to whom she had been married for 73 years had a dream.

In the dream, he saw Mawmaw. She was no longer bound to the wheelchair which she had been forced to use over the last few years, but instead was walking down the hall to the kitchen. As she went down the hall, she turned and looked at my grandfather and said: 'I'm going to make breakfast now.' When my grandfather told me about the dream, he said 'When I woke up, I thought about the dream and I knew everything was going to be all right.'

I smile even now when I think of Pawpaw's words. I know that he had never heard of Mother Julian. In the Christian tradition within which he had been brought up in, he would not have read *The Revelations of Divine Love*. And yet, he was echoing the sentiments of the fourteenth-century mystic when, after great suffering, it came to her that 'all will be well and all will be well and all manner of things will be well'.[29] How can it be? Perhaps we find some clue in the last book of the Bible, the Revelation to John, which, in spite of our traveller's misgivings at the beginning of this book, does have more to offer than strange stories about dragons and beasts with ten horns and seven heads! In this apocalypse, John (writing from the Isle of Patmos) has a vision of a new heaven and new earth where death will be no more and mourning and crying and pain will be no more. He wrote:

Then I saw a new heaven and a new earth; for the first heaven and the first earth had passed away, and the sea was no more. And I saw the holy city, the new Jerusalem, coming down out of heaven from God,

prepared as a bride adorned for her husband. And I heard a loud voice
from the throne saying:
'See, the throne of God is among mortals.
He will dwell with them as their God;
they will be his peoples, and God will himself be with them;
he will wipe away every tear from their eyes.
Death will be no more;
mourning and crying and pain will be no more,
for the first things have passed away.
And the one who was seated on the throne said, 'See I am making all
things new'. Also he said, 'Write this, for these words are trustworthy
and true.' Then he said to me, 'It is done! I am the Alpha and the
Omega, the beginning and the end. To the thirsty I will give water as a
gift from the spring of the water of life. Those who conquer will inherit
these things, and I will be their God and they will be my children.'
(Revelation 21.1–7)

While reminding us of God's presence and care for all creation now,
John's vision seems to be reiterating that our place of belonging in God
is experienced now and in the future too. While people may experience
a longing to know and to be known by God, real belonging is beyond
what we know and understand now. There are no words for love which
calls and embraces now and always; language breaks down. Yet, as I have
tried to show throughout this book, the union, or communion, in Christ
which Christian spirituality points to reaches beyond the bounds of local
church community life or even denominational life. Indeed, Christian
spirituality holds to a belief and experience in a God who is love, revealed and made known through the life, death and resurrection of Jesus
Christ. It does this while continuing to search for God in the belief that
God, too, is searching and longing for the fulfilment of all God's purpose
in us. Essentially, Christian spirituality is nurtured through life within
community while still longing for a different kind of community: a community participating in God's love . . . now and forevermore.

Draw your own conclusions

Reflect on the idea of 'active waiting'. What do you think Thomas Kelly
means when he says that we must learn to live in the 'passive voice'?

How did Martin Luther King's non-violent approach demonstrate the
practice of 'active waiting'?

What do you think Dorothy Day meant when she said, 'we have all known the long loneliness'? What might be the outworking for Christian spirituality if 'the only solution is love and that love comes in community'?

Think about the idea of the 'communion of saints'. How might a belief in participation in a larger community shape an individual's approach to Christian spirituality? How might it enlarge the understanding of God in Christian spirituality?

Further reading

Richard Bauckham (1999) (ed.), *God Will Be All In All: The Eschatology of Jürgen Moltmann*, Edinburgh: T&T Clark.

Richard Bauckham and Trevor Hart (1999), *Hope Against Hope: Christian Eschatology in Contemporary Context*, London: Darton, Longman & Todd.

Paul S. Fiddes (2000), *The Promised End: Eschatology in Theology and Literature*, Oxford: Blackwell.

John Macquarrie (1978), *Christian Hope*, Oxford: Mowbray.

Jürgen Moltmann (1967), *Theology of Hope*, London: SCM Press.

Jürgen Moltmann (1996), *The Coming of God*, London: SCM Press.

Notes

1 I am indebted to E. Glenn Hinson for this phrase.

2 Henri J. M. Nouwen (1980), *Reaching Out*, Glasgow: William Collins, p. 36.

3 V. H. Vanstone (1982), *The Stature of Waiting*, London: Darton, Longman & Todd, pp. 7ff.

4 Henri J. M. Nouwen (1987), 'A Spirituality of Waiting: Being Alert to God's Presence in Our Lives', Active Waiting, *Weavings, A Journal of the Christian Spiritual Life*, January/February, II, no.1, p. 15.

5 Nouwen, 'A Spirituality of Waiting', p. 15.

6 Evelyn Underhill (1934), *The School of Charity*, London: Longmans Green and Co., p. 62.

7 Underhill, *School of Charity*, p. 62.

8 Thomas Kelly (1941), *A Testament of Devotion*, New York: Harper and Brothers, p. 47.

9 Kelly, *Testament of Devotion*, p. 61.

10 See Karen E. Smith (2004), 'Dorothy Day: An Ordinary Saint?' in *Perspectives in Religious Studies*, Vol. 3, Number 1 (Spring), pp. 71–82.

11 Dorothy Day (1952), *The Long Loneliness*, New York: Harper & Row, p. 286.

12 Day, *The Long Loneliness*, p. 25.

13 Day, *The Long Loneliness*, p. 39.

14 Day, *The Long Loneliness*, p. 41.

15 Day, *The Long Loneliness*, p. 134.

16 Day, *The Long Loneliness*, p. 116.

17 Day, *The Long Loneliness*, p. 138.

18 Day, *The Long Loneliness*, p. 165.

19 Day, *The Long Loneliness*, p. 166.

20 Jim Forest, *Dorothy Day – A Saint for Our Age?* (Presented at the Dorothy Day Centenary Conference, Marquette University, 10 October 1997) online at www.catholicworker.org/dorothyday p. 49.

21 Dorothy Day (1963), *Loaves and Fishes*, New York: Orbis, p. 215.

22 James Melvin Washington (ed.) (1986), *A Testament of Hope: The Essential Writings and Speeches of Martin Luther King, Jr.*, New York: HarperCollins, p. xvi.

23 King's speech taken from the US Constitution online website at http://www.usconstitution.net/dream.html, accessed 17 March 2007.

24 Walter Rauschenbusch (1907), *Christianity and the Social Crisis*, Norwood, Mass: The Macmillan Company, p. 65.

25 King, 'Pilgrimage to NonViolence', in *A Testament of Hope*, p. 38.

26 King, 'Stride Toward Freedom', in *A Testament of Hope*, p. 486.

27 E. Glenn Hinson (1994), 'On Coping With Your Anger', in Anger, *Weavings, A Journal of the Christian Spiritual Life*, Vol. IX, no. 2, March/April, p. 37.

28 King, 'Stride Toward Freedom', in *A Testament of Hope*, p. 485.

29 Julian of Norwich, *Revelation of Divine Love*, ed. Halcyon Backhouse, London: Hodder & Stoughton, p. 56.

Glossary of Christian Writers and Devotional Texts

Athanasius (*c.* 296–373) The Bishop of Alexandria who attended the Council of Nicea in 325 and stood firmly against Arianism. He wrote the *Life of St Antony* which was intended to promote the monastic life and present Antony as the 'ideal' monk.

Augustine (354–430) A theologian and Bishop of Hippo whose writings shaped western theology. The *Confessions* offers the reader insight into his understanding of Christian experience.

Bernard of Clairvaux (1090–1153) Abbott and founder of the Cistercian monastery at Clairvaux, he became involved in many ecclesiastical and political debates and was a leading and influential leader in Europe in his time. Many of his sermons, letters and treatises have been collected and published, among them *On the Love of God* and *The Steps of Humility.*

Bloom, Anthony (1914–2003) Archbishop of the Russian Orthodox Church in Britain from 1962 to 1974, he wrote 12 books including *Meditations on a Theme: A Spiritual Journey, School for Prayer,* and *Living Prayer.* For more information and a list of all of his writings see http://www.metropolit-anthony.orc.ru/eng/eng_publ.htm. Also see the Orthodox website: http://www.orthodox.clara.net/index.html

Bonhoeffer, Dietrich (1906–45) A German theologian, spiritual writer and a leader in the German Protestant Church's struggle against Nazism, Bonhoeffer was arrested, imprisoned and died in a Nazi prisoner of war camp. For those beginning to study his spirituality see: *Letters and Papers From Prison, Life Together* and *The Cost of Discipleship. A Testament to Freedom: The Essential Writings of Dietrich Bonhoeffer* has been edited by Geoffrey B. Kelly and F. Burton Nelson. Website for the International Dietrich Bonhoeffer Society: http://www.dbonhoeffer.org

Bunyan, John (1628–88) A Puritan writer and preacher, he was arrested and imprisoned for preaching and spent many years in Bedford gaol. He is best remembered for his allegory of the Christian life, *Pilgrim's Progress*, and his autobiography *Grace Abounding*. To read this online see http://www.gutenberg.org/etext/654

Cassian, John (*c.* 360–435) A theologian and monk, he brought to western Christianity many of the traditions and wisdom of the Desert Fathers. His works include: the *Institutes* and the *Conferences*. To read these online see: http://www.newadvent.org/fathers/3507.htm and http://www.newadvent.org/fathers/3508.htm

Catherine of Siena (1340–80) A lay affiliate of the Dominican Order, she lived at home instead of in the convent and practised a strict ascetic way of life. She wrote *Dialogue of Divine Providence*. The letters of Catherine may be read at: http://www.gutenberg.org/etext/7403

The Cloud of Unknowing A fourteenth-century mystical work, the authorship of which is unknown. It draws on the writings of a fifth-century writer known as Pseudo-Dionysius the Areopagite and promotes the idea that those who want to discover God through contemplation will find that God is 'known' in 'not knowing'. For an edition online see http://www.ccel.org/ccel/anonymous2/cloud.html

Day, Dorothy (1897–1980) The founder of the Catholic Worker Movement, she wrote many articles and books mainly relating to issues of social justice and peace. Some may be read online at: http://www.catholicworker.org/dorothyday/ddbiography. Her autobiography is entitled *The Long Loneliness*.

Desert Mothers and Fathers Third-century men and women who fled to the desert in Egypt in order to devote themselves to live in solitude and prayer.

Fox, George (1624–91) The founder of the Religious Society of Friends (commonly known as the Quakers). Some of his letters offering advice on the Christian way have been collected and published and his *Journal* offers insight into his understanding of Christian devotion.

Francis of Assisi (1181–1226) The founder of the Roman Catholic religious order known as the Order of Friars Minor, more commonly known as the Franciscans. He is remembered for his life of poverty and love for creation.

Hammarskjöld, Dag (1905–61) A Swedish diplomat and the second secretary-general of the United Nations, he was awarded the Nobel Peace prize in 1961. His private journal was published posthumously as *Markings*.

Herbert, George (1593–1633) Poet, orator and priest in the Church of England, he served as rector of the church at Bemerton near Salisbury. He wrote many poems and hymns including *The Temple: Sacred Poems and Private Ejaculations*. He also wrote *A Priest to the Temple* (or *The Country Parson*) which offered practical advice to ministers in rural parishes.

Hügel, Baron Friedrich von (1852–1925) A Roman Catholic philosopher and writer. He was a leader in the so-called Catholic Modernist movement which sought to engage Christian faith with questions related to science, history, philosophy and psychology. He never earned a university degree, but he was awarded honorary doctorates by the University of Oxford and St Andrews University and to the latter he bequeathed his library and manuscript papers. He is best remembered for his spiritual advice to many friends, including Evelyn Underhill. Many of his letters were published posthumously: *Selected Letters, 1896–1924*, *Letters from Baron Friedrich von Hügel to a Niece*, *Spiritual Counsels* and *Letters of Baron Friedrich von Hügel*. Other published works include: *The Mystical Element of Religion*, *Eternal Life*, *Essays and Addresses* and *The Reality of God and Religion and Agnosticism*.

Ignatius of Loyola (1491–1556) The founder and first Superior General of a Roman Catholic religious order known as the Society of Jesus (commonly known as Jesuits). His *Spiritual Exercises* was originally written as a guide for prayer and meditation on a month-long retreat. However, the Ignatian method has been adapted and used for encouraging meditation and contemplative prayer.

John of the Cross (1542–91) A Roman Catholic mystical writer and member of the Carmelite order, he worked with St Teresa of Avila to reform the Carmelites. He wrote many works and is especially remembered for the *Dark Night of the Soul* and *Ascent of Mount Carmel*. Several of his works may be read online at: http://www.ccel.org/j/john_cross/?show=works

Julian of Norwich (*c.* 1342–*c.* 1416) Probably a Benedictine nun of the house at Carrow, near Norwich, she lived for much of her life in seclusion in an anchorage in the churchyard of St Julian at Norwich. During a severe illness at the age of 30, she had a series of visions or *showings*, which she later reflected on in her work, *Revelations of Divine Love*.

Kelly, Thomas (1893–1941) An American Quaker and writer. He taught philosophy at Haverford College in Philadelphia and wrote *A Testament of Devotion*.

King, Martin Luther (1929–68) A Baptist minister and leader of the American Civil Rights Movement, he is considered one of America's greatest orators and was awarded the Nobel Peace Prize in 1964. His autobiography was published under the title *Stride Toward Freedom*. His works have been collected and edited by James Melvin Washington in *A Testament of Hope: The Essential Writings and Speeches of Martin Luther King, Jr.*

Lawrence, Brother (*c.* 1605–91) (baptized as Nicolas Herman) A soldier who became a Carmelite lay brother in 1649. He worked in the kitchen of the monastery in Paris and was known for his simple prayers and insistence that it was possible to know the presence of God anywhere, even in the noise and clatter of a kitchen.

Lewis, C. S. (1898–1963) He taught at the University of Oxford and is remembered for his writings on medieval literature, Christian apologetics, literary criticism and fiction. His autobiography, *Surprised by Joy*, describes his experience of faith. He wrote many books including the popular children's series, *The Chronicles of Narnia*.

Luther, Martin (1483–1546) A German monk and theologian, who became a Protestant reformer. Many of his writings including prayers and sermons may be read online at: http://www.iclnet.org/pub/resources/text/wittenberg/wittenberg-home.html

Merton, Thomas (1915–68) A Trappist monk and one of the foremost Catholic writers of the twentieth century, he wrote over 50 books and many articles and poems. His autobiography is entitled *The Seven Storey Mountain* (published in Britain under the title *Elected Silence*). Other well-known works include: *New Seeds of Contemplation*, *Conjectures of a Guilty Bystander*, *Contemplative Prayer* and *Thoughts in Solitude*. Website: http://www.merton.org/

Newman, J. H. (1801–90) A leader of the nineteenth-century Oxford Movement, he left the Anglican Church and was received into the Roman Catholic Church in 1845. His spirituality was nourished by the writings of the Church Fathers and he encouraged the idea of the growth and development of Christian doctrine.

Nouwen, Henri (1932–96) A twentieth-century Dutch Catholic priest and writer who taught at Harvard and Yale before joining a L'Arche community in Canada. He wrote over 40 books and many articles. Some of his best-known devotional writings are: *Reaching Out, The Wounded Healer, The Way of the Heart* and *The Return of the Prodigal Son*. Website: http://www.henrinouwen.org/

Origen (*c.* 185– *c.* 254) A theologian, and spiritual writer from Alexandria, he wrote many letters and treatises. His work *On Prayer* may be read online at http://www.ccel.org/ccel/origen/prayer.html

Pascal, Blaise (1623–1662) A French mathematician and theologian, he was influenced by Augustinian thought and defended the Jansenist cause at Port Royal. He had a religious experience in 1654 which he recorded in the *Memorial*. His main devotional work is known as *Pensées*.

Patrick, St (*c.* 390–*c.* 460) Born in Britain, he undertook a mission to Ireland about AD 430. He is identified with the Celtic tradition of spirituality.

Rauschenbusch, Walter (1861–1918) An American Baptist theologian and leader of the Social Gospel Movement. After serving as a pastor among the poor in an area known as 'Hell's Kitchen' in New York, he taught at the Rochester Theological Seminary. He wrote *Christianity and the Social Crisis, Christianizing the Social Order* and *Theology for the Social Gospel*.

Roger, Brother (1915–2005) Baptized Roger Louis Schütz-Marsauche, he was the founder of the Taizé community. This is an international ecumenical monastic community which was founded in France in 1940. Brother Roger wrote many books on themes related to the Christian life. Website: http://www.taize.fr/en

Rolle, Richard (*c.* 1300–49) An English mystical writer, he was born and lived for most of his life in Yorkshire. He lived as a hermit and spent the last years of his life near a convent of Cistercian nuns at Hampole. He wrote a number of works, but is best remembered for *The Fire of Love* and *The Mending of Life*.

Romero, Oscar (1917–80) A Roman Catholic priest in El Salvador who became the fourth Archbishop of San Salvador, he embraced liberation theology and was an outspoken advocate for the poor and oppressed. He was killed in a church service in 1980. A number of biographies have been written. His work may be explored in: *The Violence of Love* and *Voice of the Voiceless: Four Pastoral Letters and Other Statements*.

Steere, Douglas (1901–95) An American Quaker, he taught at Haverford College between 1928 and 1964. Douglas Steere attended the Second Vatican Council, corresponded regularly with Thomas Merton, and kept in contact with many significant religious thinkers of his day. He wrote books and articles on the spiritual life including *On Listening to Another*. *Love at the Heart of Things: A Biography of Douglas V. Steere*, has been written by E. Glenn Hinson.

Teilhard de Chardin, Pierre (1881–1955) A French Jesuit priest, palae-ontologist and philosopher, Teilhard wrote of the development of the universe from creation to what he described as the Omega point in the future. His ideas are presented in *The Phenomenon of Man*. His spirituality may be explored in *The Divine Milieu*, *The Hymn of the Universe* and *Letters from a Traveller 1923–1955*.

Teresa of Avila (1515–82) A Spanish Carmelite and mystical writer, with John of the Cross she called for reform of the Carmelite order and established houses that were based on the primitive rule. In her writings she outlined various stages of prayer moving towards mystical union with God. She wrote a number of works including: *The Interior Castle*, *The Way of Perfection*, and the *Life*. These may be read online at: http://www.ccel.org/ccel/teresa/castle2.html

Thérèse of Lisieux (1873–97) A Carmelite sometimes known as the Little Flower of Jesus, she emphasized simplicity of heart and holiness of life. She is remembered for her emphasis on 'the little way' because for her perfection was reached through the completion of small tasks. Her spiritual autobiography is *The Story of A Soul*.

Underhill, Evelyn (1875–1941) A mystical writer who published 39 books and more than 350 articles and reviews, she was encouraged by Baron Friedrich von Hügel who was her spiritual director. Her writings include:

Mysticism: The Nature and Development of Spiritual Consciousness and *A Life of Prayer.* A complete list of her writings may be found at the website for the Evelyn Underhill Association: http://www.evelynunderhill.org/index.htm

Vanier, Jean (b. 1928) The founder of the L'Arche communities, he has written many books and lectured on themes such as peace, prayer and community.

Weil, Simone (1909–43) A French philosopher, religious thinker, and social and political activist. Most of her work was published posthumously. An introduction to her spirituality may be found in *Waiting On God.*

Woolman, John (1720–72) An American Quaker who spoke out against slavery and other social injustices, he advocated a life of simplicity and care for all living things. His story is recorded in his *Journal.*

Sources and Acknowledgements

I am pleased to record my gratitude to the following publishers for permission to quote from other published texts:

Wendell Berry (2004), *Hannah Coulter*, Emeryville CA: Shoemaker & Hoard, pp.93–4. Copyright© 2004 by Wendell Berry from *Hannah Coulter*. Reprinted by permission of Shoemaker & Hoard.

T. S. Eliot (1944), 'Little Gidding', in *Four Quartets*, London: Faber & Faber, p.48. Reprinted by permission of Faber & Faber.

Thomas Merton (1958), *Thoughts in Solitude*, Tunbridge Wells: Burns and Oates. Reprinted by permission of Continuum International Publishing Group.

Simone Weil (1951), *Waiting on God*, Glasgow: Harper Collins, pp.25, 66–7. Used by permission of Zondervan, copyright © 1988.

Permission has been requested to reproduce the 'I Have a Dream' speech by Martin Luther King Jr.

Index of Scriptural References

Index of Names and Subjects